American
Hauntings

American Hauntings

Mary Beth Sammons
Robert Edwards

BARNES
& NOBLE
BOOKS

NEW YORK

Copyright © 2005 by Barnes & Noble Publishing, Inc.

Book design by Nicola Ferguson

ISBN 0-7607-6293-7

Printed and bound in the United States of America

10   9   8   7   6   5   4   3   2   1

Contents

PART IV Meet the Rich and Famous
WHO'VE CHARTED THE COURSE FOR CELEBRITY GHOSTS

Introduction

Everyone loves a good ghost story. And just about everyone seems to have one.

During the months we spent researching this book and interviewing ghost hunters and historians, we had no trouble uncovering literally hundreds of documented stories about ghosts and hauntings in America.

We became fascinated not only by the sheer volume of ghost stories out there, but by the firsthand accounts, legends, literature, and dramatic tales surrounding the world of ghosts. They seemed to pop up everywhere we looked. Our professional and often personal conversations began to buzz with our quest to learn more about the authentic roots of America's ghost stories. We found ourselves turning to friends, colleagues, and sometimes even strangers, and asking the question: "Do you have a ghost or a haunting story to share?"

The resounding answer was, "yes." From students who swore they'd heard unexplained noises in classrooms, to office workers who spouted off scary tales from the urban-legend front, to historians who recorded sightings at battlefields and boarded-up mansions, to hotel owners and innkeepers, the stories were neverending.

American Hauntings is a collection of what we believe are some of the best stories that bring to life some of America's most talked about haunted places. It's a book filled with documented sagas of souls trapped between this world and the afterlife, and the colorful spirits who have made their presence known.

It's also a rich travelogue that takes readers behind the scenes of some of the most haunted places in America (more than one hundred of them). We've broken the chapters down into places where spirits have haunted and continue to haunt today-hotels, inns, B& B's, plantations, mansions, hospitals, prisons, schools, theaters, landmarks, and outdoor locales including battlefields, lighthouses, and cemeteries. We take readers to some of the best known and most colorful travel destinations: from the Hotel Del Coronado, one of America's most beautiful resorts, to the ghosts of the Civil War, to haunted houses in Indiana. The ghosts are among us everywhere and we introduce you to them in schools and universities, local theaters, historic lighthouses, four-star hotels, hospitals, cemeteries, and in some of America's most famed monuments.

What we know to be true is that haunted places have very special personalities and fascinating histories. We hope our stories inspire your thirst for the supernatural and give you a closer glimpse into the phenomenon of ghosts and hauntings. As you read the selections, we hope you enjoy them as much as we enjoyed learning about these chilling and thrilling tales for the first time.

Happy hauntings,
—The Editors

SO WHAT ARE GHOSTS?

Are there really ghosts? We are convinced from the more than 100 tales that we've collected, and from the dozens of others (too many to put in this book) that we were told, that one thing is for certain: There are many ghost sightings that have been documented by reliable sources.

We've all seen ghosts depicted in movies, read stories of their unnerving activities, and have seen television shows and documentaries sensationalizing them.

But what are ghosts? No one knows for certain. Some experts believe ghosts are a popular phenomena in our culture because everyone loves a good ghost story-and the spiritual reassurance that a belief in a neverending existence brings them.

We've also discovered that people seek haunted locations for myriad reasons: from the thrill and sensationalism to more profound goals. More and more people are seeking a deeper meaning to life itself. Still others seek out haunted places and ghost stories because they've lost a loved one, and they desperately want proof that life transcends death. Encountering a ghost, they believe, gives them that proof.

Certainly, hauntings by ghosts and spirits have been in existence throughout history. The ancient literature of Assyria and Babylon describes such beings as ghostly wanderers. These wanderers are ghosts who are looking for something to put them to rest, or are spirits, more apt to be of evil nature than good, with a specific purpose in mind. In Greek and Roman literature, there are references to ghosts appearing and demanding to be properly buried, or some returning to give advice or warnings to the living.

Today's common belief is that a spirit has an overwhelming feeling for a person or place and does not want to leave them. Spirits also have strong attachments to physical properties, of which they can't seem to let go; some ghosts appear following accidents, suicide, and murder because the spirit was unprepared to cross over and leave this earthly plane.

Ghosts and apparitions can come in many forms. Ghosts are generally a visual image of a human being in human form, perhaps transparent, that has passed on and comes back to make an appearance. Apparitions are an unusual visual appearance or physical phenomena, one that is not necessarily in human form—more often seen as patches of light, passing shadows, even streaks of light or an orb, a floating luminescent sphere.

Poltergeists are a different concept than ghosts and apparitions. Many experts believe poltergeists are not spirits returning to this world but bundles of psychic and telekinetic energy created by living humans or some non-human source. The word "poltergeist" means "noisy ghost," and can include such occurrences as flying objects, spontaneous fires, levitations, the knocking, opening, and closing of doors, and turning things off and on. Poltergeists are also usually of a more destructive nature than ghosts.

While researching the stories for this book it became clear that some of the hauntings are by ghosts, some by apparitions, other by poltergeists, sometimes alone, sometimes a little of each, and sometimes all three at once.

PART I

This Old House

AMERICA'S MOST HAUNTED

MANSIONS, HOTELS, GUEST HOUSES,

PLANTATIONS, INNS, AND B&B'S

And now for a thrilling new dimension to your ghost musings. Whether it's armchair travel or real sight-seeing adventures, an exploration of America's old houses and mansions, hotels and inns, is an ideal way to experience mysterious encounters with ghosts.

Offering a chilling blend of travel and history, this chapter is spiced with firsthand accounts of unusual encounters that occurred in the various locations. With each selection, you'll be transported back to some of the most fascinating moments in American history. You'll encounter ghosts from pre-Civil War America and from the Old West, ghosts who hail from Victorian manors and from Southern plantations, and from the people who helped shape our country's history.

Some of the haunted locations were once private homes where human tragedy, failed romance, untimely death, and betrayal once occurred. Others were buildings where historical incidents took place-usually violent-including soldiers, slaves, and other victims of history.

One common theme runs through the hauntings. They are all located in places that have housed either great happiness or tremendous loss. It is this highly charged emotional environment that seems to call back the ghosts of the people whose stories still beckon to be told.

You'll meet the ghost of Kate Morgan at the Hotel Del Coronado in San Diego, California, and "Aunt Nora" at the Poplar Grove Plantation on the Cape Fear River. You'll also read about haunted dwellings in the Midwest and Chicago, where the Windy City offers some of the most fascinating ghosts and spirits blowing through the nation. Florida resorts, Arizona retreats, and even Alaska are all home to some of the spookiest places in America. And each haunting reveals a tale of tortured lovers, vengeful siblings, battle-scarred soldiers, and more chilling detail to recount.

So step into the living rooms, dining halls, and guesthouses of some of the most stately mansions, beautifully maintained inns, exquisitely restored hotels, and historical dwellings in the United States and experience their eerie ghost stories for yourselves. You are sure to be intrigued-and perhaps enticed to arrange for a tour or an overnight stay yourself.

Hotels and Resorts

The Alaskan Hotel
Juneau, Alaska

Ghost of the Gold Rush

It was October 3, 1880, when Joe Juneau and Richard Harris and their Tlingit Indian guide found gold in the Silver Bow Basin, in a stream they appropriately named Gold Creek. This event spawned a continent-wide gold rush to this largely untapped section of the world. Over the years, many people came to the wilds of Alaska searching for this precious metal.

But beyond the gold, the hills and towns are alive with ghosts.

One of the liveliest hauntings is at the Alaskan Hotel in the state capital of Juneau, a town of about 31,000 people. The hotel, which is Juneau's oldest continuously operating hotel, was built in 1913 and is now on the National Registry of Historic Places. It was originally set up as a bordello to serve the gold miners. It was quite common during the gold rush days that men significantly outnumbered women, and the houses of prostitution were very popular places.

The legend is that the ghost that haunts the Alaskan Hotel is that of a woman driven to prostitution when her husband never returned from the mines and she found herself penniless. After she became a prostitute, her husband returned and was furious. He then killed her.

Today, she is folklore among the townsfolk of Juneau. Some say that they see an apparition of a woman standing at the top of the stairway that they believe is the murdered woman. Rooms 218 and 219 of the hotel are said to be especially haunted, with cold spells and a reported feeling of uneasiness from guests who stay there. Many feel like someone is touching them when they sleep. It is not unusual for guests to insist on being removed from the rooms.

Juneau was originally founded and thrived during the gold rush days. The town was originally called "Harrisburgh." No one knows exactly how the town's name changed, but, Richard Harris was not a particularly popular person, and after Joe Juneau bought a couple of rounds of drinks the locals decided to change the name.

THE ALASKAN HOTEL & BAR
167 SOUTH FRANKLIN STREET
JUNEAU, ALASKA 99801
(907) 586-1000

HISTORY OF THE GOLD RUSH

More than one hundred years ago the great Klondike Gold Rush focused attention on Alaska and Canada's Yukon Territory. Ships flooded the Inside Passage and Skagway became a bustling city of 20,000 people. From Skagway thousands of boomers climbed Chilcoot Pass with a tremendous amount of food and provisions, as the Canadian authorities would not let anyone into Canada without a year's provisions. The great gold rush focused on the Dawson City area in the Yukon Territory of Canada, but there was a lot of overflow down the Yukon River and across the Canadian line into what is today the state of Alaska.

HOTEL MONTE VISTA,
FLAGSTAFF, ARIZONA

Lights, Camera . . . Ghosts: Home to More than 100 Hollywood Western Epics, Flagstaff Hotel Continues to Host Many Other-Worldly Guests

Bing Crosby, Jane Russell, Gary Cooper, Spencer Tracy, and John Wayne may have put the Monte Vista Hotel on the Big Screen. But it's the phantom of a bellboy with a mysterious woman, and the ghost of a bank robber who today capture the attention and share the limelight at this beautiful historic Flagstaff, Arizona, hotel.

Opened on New Year's Day in 1927, the Flagstaff Hotel was a popular spot for Hollywood guests during the 1940s and 1950s, and it has been the scene for more than one hundred westerns. The hotel quickly became a must-go destination for tourists and glamorous people from all over the world. It also became a favorite place for locals to hang out. For many years, the phrase "Meet me at the Monte V" was heard all over town.

Today, the Hotel has captured interest as one of the most haunted in America and its ghosts have been spotlighted on several television shows. The many spirits that roam the property make noise, knock on doors, move furniture, and knock things down, said Chris Hartzog, the front-desk manager.

"Everybody that works here is just kind of used to it," Hartzog said. "In fact, it's kind of a joke with us. If something's missing and it shows up days later, we just kind of say, 'Oh, it was a ghost.'"

Even famous folks have reported these ghosts. In the late 1950s, actor John Wayne reported seeing a friendly ghost in his hotel room. The ghost story quickly spread, but now more than fifty similar stories circulate. In nearly every case, the ghosts are friendly and well behaved.

Dozens of guests over the years have reported an annoying bellboy, who taunts them by knocking on doors then vanishing. Sometimes he is joined by the ghost of a woman, and they are seen near the Zane Grey Suite.

Another ghost is thought to be that of a former bank

robber who haunts the saloon. According to local legend, in 1970, three men robbed a nearby bank and then stopped in the lounge for a drink to celebrate—even though one of them had been shot during their escape. While having his drink, the wounded man died. Now, his spirit continues to haunt the saloon—and the bar stool where he sat when he died.

Other Monte Vista ghosts include two murdered prostitutes who hang out in the pool hall and lounge, and a boarder in Room 220 who died in the 1980s during his stay at the hotel. His spirit apparently overstayed its welcome.

Guests have complained of coughing and other noises coming from Room 220, even when no one is staying there. In Room 305, there is often an attractive female ghost sitting in the rocking chair. On the third floor, a man endlessly paces inside one of the guest rooms. He is often heard coughing and clearing his throat.

The Hotel Monte Vista is one of the few American hotels built through public subscription. In 1924, V. M. Slipher, an astronomer at Lowell Observatory, spearheaded a local fundraising campaign that resulted in a city-voted ordinance establishing a municipal bond, held by the citizens of Flagstaff themselves, to build the Hotel Monte Vista.

Tourism was a growing business in Flagstaff, and the town's leaders were concerned that not enough lodging was available to keep visitors in town long enough to spend their money. Slipher not only pushed the idea through, he also designed and oversaw much of the actual construction. Completed in 1927, the Hotel is today fully restored to its original splendor and beauty.

In 1927, Mary Costigan became the first American woman

to be granted a radio-broadcasting license, and her three-hour radio show aired daily from her second floor studio at the Hotel Monte Vista, Room 105.

After World War II, Hollywood glitterati favored the Hotel Monte Vista. The Hotel Monte Vista amassed a widespread reputation for having the best and friendliest service around. The hotel's barber was once flown to Phoenix upon special request to cut Harry Truman's hair. The president stated he wanted the best, and knew he could get it from the Hotel Monte Vista.

HOTEL MOUNT VISTA
100 N. SAN FRANCISCO ST.
FLAGSTAFF, ARIZONA 86001
(928) 779-6971

OATMAN HOTEL,
OATMAN, ARIZONA

A Hollywood Star and a Lonely Immigrant Keep Guests Spooked In Remote Arizona Mining Town

One of the most famous haunted locations along historic Route 66, the famous Chicago-Los Angeles highway, is the Oatman Hotel, located on Main Street in Oatman, Arizona. Oatman is a old mining town with about one hundred residents near the Arizona-Mexico border. Over the years, the hotel has had several different names, but it has been known as the Oatman Hotel since the 1960s.

It was at the Oatman Hotel that Carole Lombard and Clark Gable spent their wedding night on March 29, 1939. They often returned to spend quiet times, playing cards, and chatting with the locals. Guests and employees now hear laughter and whispering coming from the room where they stayed; perhaps they are recapturing happy moments from their honeymoon

Even many skeptics don't deny the existence of ghostly spirits, especially the most notorious ghost in town, "Oatie," whose antics still get the blame for most peculiar doings in town, says Tom Woodward, president of the Oatman Gold Road Chamber of Commerce. He reports,

> While I am not too much on being the spooky kind and pretty skeptical for the most part on ghost stories, there are some things here in Oatman that happen that do make you wonder. I live in an old miner's shack and there have been times that something catches me out of the corner of my eye, and I turn and look and there is nothing there. And, occasionally I get the feeling that something or someone is in the room with me, but there is no one there. Every time something seeming unexplainable will happen, old Oatie gets the blame for it.

Oatie's real name was William Ray Flour. He was a miner who came to Arizona from Ireland, and unfortunately, when he sent for his wife and two children, they perished on the trip to America.

Peg Robertson, the local wedding photographer for the Ghost Rider Gunfighter's "Shot Gun Weddings" has this to say about Oatie: "Being the good Irishman the he was, he enjoyed his drinks. He was known to get drunk at night because he missed his homeland and his ladylove so much. One night he passed out in a trash pile behind the hotel and died. His body was found two days later and buried in a shallow grave." From that time on, his ghost was given the nickname of Oatie and has remained at the hotel to this day. Oatie wanders around during the night, and has been known to play his bagpipes on numerous occasions.

Adds Robertson: "Oatie enjoys being a prankster with the locals and guests alike. He has been seen by many, many people over the years, and was even photographed. Some previous owners of the hotel had ghost experts come to the hotel, and they confirmed the presence of unusually high unexplained energy throughout the building. "

Many times, guests have checked in and gone up to their room, and in less than an hour are seen coming down the stairs on the run, their luggage in their hands, and out the front door, never to be seen again. "There are times when you swear you can hear him laughing," says Robertson.

Once, the hotel's gift shop put a life-sized doll on display. The doll was seen by hotel employees flying across the lobby on numerous occasions, even when no one was there. For months, when the shop was opened in the morning, the doll had been moved again to either the counter or leaning against the wall right next to the door.

"It was obvious that Oatie wanted that doll put out in the lobby," says Robertson. "Having a pretty good friendship with Oatie, the owner told him to find another toy to play with, and eventually he stopped."

But many of Oatie's activities are nerve-racking. According to the hotel staff, Oatie frequently hides things, moves them, and even breaks them. They say when he isn't at the bar; he's often up in his room sitting by the window in a rocking chair. Guests and staff frequently find the chair rocking by itself.

One guest reported the quilt in the room floating off the bed to the rocking chair by the window. Then the chair started rocking. Most of the employees have encountered Oatie. The most common sightings are of things flying through the air, being broken, or glass that shatters as it sits untouched.

Once a mining tent camp in the early 1900s, Oatman quickly became a flourishing gold-mining center. In 1915, two miners struck a $10 million gold find, and within a year the town's population had grown to more than 3,500. Then, just as quickly, the population declined. After a fire burned down most of the town in 1921, and before the opening of Route 66, Oatman's population plummeted to a low of fifteen residents from its peak of 10,000.

Today this four block-long authentic old western town has very few full-time residents, but it has taken on a new life as a tourist attraction. Gunfights are staged on weekends. Because of its Old West feel, Hollywood came to town to set the scene for many blockbusters including *How the West Was Won, Foxfire, and Edge of Eternity.*

And, the Oatman Hotel has become a popular tourist

attraction, thanks to Clark Gable and Oatie. These days, the Clark Gable/Carole Lombard suite is roped off as a museum. But Oatie's room remains open to inquiring guests.

THE OATMAN HOTEL

181 NORTH MAIN ST.

ROUTE 66

OATMAN, ARIZONA 86433

(602) 768-4408

CRESCENT HOTEL AND SPA
EUREKA SPRINGS, ARKANSAS

Culinary Capers and Past Life Experiences Continue to Haunt the Halls of this "Queen of the Ozarks"

When the Crescent Hotel opened in 1886, it was built to be the grandest hotel located in the Ozarks. It was also a showcase of the latest modern conveniences-central steam heat, lamps by Edison, and even a hydraulic lift elevator. The rooms were decorated with only the best furniture of the time. Guests could partake in activities such as an afternoon high tea, ballroom dancing, and horseback riding.

Today, in addition to the hotel's excellent recreational facilities, there are also ghosts. In the hotel's elaborate Crystal Dining Room, the site of many of the haunted sightings, many guests and employees have reported encountering playful spirits in Victorian formal dress. During one Christmas season, when the dining room was closed, employees arrived one morning to find that the Christmas tree and all of the packages underneath it had been moved across the room to another corner. The next morning, they found the tree and packages moved again to another part of the dining room, this time with chairs circled around it. It seems that the ghosts were very busy while everyone else was sleeping.

Early-morning surprises happen quite frequently. One time an employee awoke to find menus scattered all over the dining room, as if a brisk wind had rushed in, except that the rest of the dining room was in impeccable order. On another occasion, a waitress was looking into the huge mirror that stands between the doors from the dining room to the kitchen and saw a man and woman in Victorian garb facing each other as if in a wedding ceremony. The groom turned and made eye contact with the waitress, and then the couple faded away. The waitress promptly quit.

Over the years, several employees and guests have reported seeing a young gentleman clad in nineteenth-century-style clothing sitting near a window in the dining room; when he is approached, he says, "I saw the most beautiful woman here last night and I am waiting for her to return." Many employees of the Crescent have told of being startled by apparitions in Victorian ball attire dancing during the wee hours of the morning while the room was closed and dark.

There is also a powerful male spirit who haunts the Crescent Hotel—Michael, an Irish stonemason who worked on building the hotel in 1886. One day, during the construction, he lost his footing and fell from the roof, landing in the second floor area. Today, he plays tricks in the area of his death, which is now Room 218. He turns the lights and TV on and off, or pounds loudly on the thick walls. Sometimes, the door to the room opens and then slams shut, often locking guests inside the room. Hotel workers have to come to let the guest out of the room.

CRESCENT HOTEL AND SPA
75 PROSPECT AVENUE
EUREKA SPRINGS, ARKANSAS
(501) 253-9766

HOTEL DEL CORONADO
SAN DIEGO, CALIFORNIA

Beautiful Stranger: The Ghost of Kate Morgan and the Hotel Del Coronado

The afternoon sun washes over the grassy expanse of the Windsor Lawn, across a terrace of tables and in through the open doors of the Spa & Fitness Center at the luxurious Hotel del Coronado in the San Diego Bay. Then, suddenly, lights start flickering, doors slam-as if being pushed by an invisible force. A massage therapist struggles in the middle of a client's herbal wrap to open up a treatment table that just won't budge. Facials stop. Massages halt. Manicures melt. Exfoliations end. "Looks like Kate's back," says Meg Kruse, manager of the spa. "Whenever weird things start happening, we know someone is about to see her."

Forget that ten American presidents bedded down beneath the signature red-turreted roof. Or, that Hotel Del was the backdrop for the cinematic frolic of Jack Lemmon and Tony Curtis and the glamorous and cavorting Marilyn Monroe in *Some Like It Hot*. Or that it was also the inspiration and influence for *The Wizard of Oz* author L. Frank Baum.

It was Kate Morgan who captured and continues to inspire major headlines as the ghost who has made herself quite comfortable-and fairly active-within the walls of this nineteenth-century hotel, the crowning point of the Coronado, California, peninsula. She, and her aura, have spun a richly layered history since the day the then 24-year-old wife and beauty checked into the Hotel Del on Thursday, November 24, 1892.

One-third sun. One-third sand. One-third fairy tale. A classic historic hotel, this seaside resort was built in 1888 and designated a National Historic Landmark in 1977. Art, architecture, film, and history buffs point to the Hotel Del Coronado as one of the most prominent and historic places in the country to hang your hat.

A beautiful place to spend a few days lapping up luxury, the Hotel Del has been described as part fairy tale castle, part luxury steamship. Rich features include the Babcock & Story Bar, home to the hotel's original 46-foot, hand-carved mahogany bar that was shipped around Cape Horn in 1888, with a view of the oceanfront through palms and French doors. The Hotel also boasts a host of modern-day amenities including the revamped oceanfront spa and fitness center and proximity to the main boulevard in Coronado, Orange Avenue, which was designed to guide visitors through a picturesque downtown and deposit them at the Del's front door.

In 1885, when Midwestern businessmen Elisha Babcock and Hampton Story bought the entire uninhabited Coronado peninsula for $110,000, it was predicted that the oceanfront property would become the talk of the western world.

Despite the ambiance and smorgasbord of activities from surfing and kayaking to poolside lounging and croquet, the ghostly goings-on continue to attract attention among visitors at Hotel Del. With guests requesting Kate Morgan's room and keeping it booked year-round, hotel owners have talked about adding other activities around her aura—sleepovers in the room for teens, storytelling sessions, and so on.

No question, many of the Hotel Del guests want to know the Kate Morgan story.

Five days after Kate registered under the alias of Lottie A. Bernard from Detroit, she was found dead on a hotel exterior staircase. Because little was known about her identity, the press referred to this mysterious woman who spent five days at the Del as "the Beautiful Stranger."

Today the mystery and questions remain. Who was this beautiful stranger? According to police reports, Kate had a gunshot wound to the head, and it was assumed she had taken her own life. But no one has ever been completely sure that is true. Others argue that her husband, Tom, murdered her.

Guests and employees alike have tried to answer the question: "Why does Kate Morgan's spirit remain at the Del?"

Some think she is still waiting for her husband Tom to join her. Others believe that without family and a permanent home, she has nowhere else to go.

Still others believe Kate Morgan doesn't want to leave the Del because she likes "living" there, says Hotel Del historian Christine Donahue.

According to the Kate legend, Tom and Kate Morgan were a married couple who rode the trains in the late 1800s. Their occupation: con artists. Kate was apparently very attractive, and would lure men into a game of cards with her "brother" (Tom), so that they could prove their worth. Tom would swindle them out of whatever money they were willing to part with, and this is how the Morgans made their living.

In November of 1892, however, Kate discovered she was pregnant and wanted to stop the train racket and settle down. While the two were riding towards San Diego, they had an argument because Tom did not want to change his lifestyle. Tom disembarked at either Los Angeles or Orange County. He was supposed to meet Kate in San Diego for Thanksgiving.

Kate continued on to San Diego and checked into the Hotel Del Coronado under the name "Lottie Anderson Bernard." There she waited for Tom, but Thanksgiving came and went with no sign of him. During this time, Kate complained to various staff members of feeling ill and reports of the time indicate that she was looking pale. It is suspected that she performed an abortion on herself.

It is known that while Kate was waiting for her missing husband, she ventured into the city and bought a gun. It was shortly after this that Kate was found shot in the head on some outside steps leading down to the beach, an apparent suicide.

Today, determined to experience the legend of Kate Morgan, guests book Room 3327, where Kate Morgan stayed, almost a year in advance, says Lauren Ash Donoho, director of public relations for the Hotel Del. The most common incidents they find are strange breezes, ghostly noises, and the pale figure of a young lady walking in a black lace dress. One time, a group of parapsychologists took more than thirty-seven abnormal readings in a single day. Guests in the room Kate stayed in have experienced oppressive feelings and have seen curtains moving even though the windows are closed. Other people swear they have heard murmurings coming from somewhere in the room. Kate's ghost has also been seen walking down hallways of the hotel and standing at windows.

An electrician has said that the light over the steps where Kate died will not stay lit. The bulb is replaced constantly, but the light always winks out. A guest also claims that while he was staying in one of the haunted rooms, he saw a face on the television (which was turned off at the time). Two hotel employees verified this sighting.

"A lot of guests who come in here for massages or spa treatments, are by nature sensitive to the psychic," says Hotel Del spa manager Kruse. "And, they all say there is an incredible phenomenon going on here. They say they have felt or seen Kate and know she is here. I don't believe or disbelieve, but I know there is a lot of psychic action going on here. And, the guests tell me they've seen or felt Kate."

HOTEL DEL CORONADO
1500 ORANGE AVENUE
CORONADO, CALIFORNIA 92118
(800) 468-3533 OR (619) 435-6611

A Brook Runs Through It: From *Ripley's Believe It or Not* to Dozens of Friendly Ghosts, Brookdale Lodge Holds a Mysterious and Rich Past

Home to the most glamorous events and fancy parties, and host to Hollywood stars, music celebrities, and a U.S. president, Brookdale Lodge boasts a *Ripley's Believe It or Not* feature, and also fifty friendly ghosts who continue to command center stage in front of modern-day guests.

Nestled deep in the redwood forests of the Santa Cruz Mountains, the Brookdale Lodge was originally built in 1870 as the headquarters of the Grover Lumber Mill. Shortly afterward, it was converted into campgrounds and a hotel.

But, it is the natural brook that runs through its dining room that has made the Brookdale Lodge world famous and earned it Ripley's acclaim. Through the years, the Santa Cruz-area resort has hosted a number of notable guests including President Herbert Hoover, Mae West, Marilyn Monroe, Tyrone Power, Joan Crawford, Rita Hayward, and neighbors Shirley Temple and Johnny Weissmuller, who lived nearby and dined there frequently.

Brookdale Lodge was also a popular setting for bands and singers of the swing era. At least three songs were written about the lodge, including: "My Brookdale Hideaway," "A Place Known as Brookdale," and "Beautiful Brookdale Lodge."

Today's visitors find the same refreshing and delightful experience of dining indoors beside the gentle brook in this unique and rustic setting. But, they also are entertained by the visions of the past, who make themselves known in present-day ghost sightings. The most common is the ghost of Sarah Logan, the niece of the lodge owner, who, in a formal dress, runs across the lobby, then disappears into thin air. Sarah is reported to have drowned in the dining room brook during the lodge's shadier times-during the 1940s, when booze and gangsters became familiar fixtures at Brookdale. During those days, the lodge had secret passageways and hidden rooms, and there were rumors of mobsters having buried a body or two under the floor. But, the capper for this shady era was the tragic story of the niece.

Clad in a 1940s-style white-and-blue Sunday dress, Sarah has been spotted numerous times walking through the lobby or near the fireplace between the lounge and the Brook Room. She's also been seen sitting quietly beside the fire in the Fireside Room, or playing on the balcony of the Brook Room, in an area that is off-limits to guests.

The crying Sarah has approached guests, asking for help finding her mother. Then, she disappears. Psychics speculate that a ghostly woman, sometimes seen walking above the brook as if supported by a bridge, is the mother of Sarah, returning to look for her daughter.

Beyond Sarah and her mother, there have been other paranormal activities at the Brookdale. In the Mermaid Room, visitors have experienced hearing voices, the clinking of glasses, and the sound of soft music. The jukebox in the room turns itself on and off. Same in the Brook Room, where big band music has been heard playing faintly. Doors slam late at night and strange smells and crowd noises give the sense the room is full of people, even when it is empty.

The smell of gardenias often permeates the area near the Brook Room at night, even though there are no gardenias in the hotel. Big band music has also been heard playing faintly in the Fireside Room and in the Pool Room. People have also reported cold spots, presences, and even being touched by unseen forces in the Pool Room. Ghostly ballroom dancers swirl around the room as they float by.

In other parts of the hotel, doors slam and footsteps are heard late at night in empty rooms. The footsteps are particularly loud in the second floor conference room. Many have reported strange smells and having a sense that the conference room is full of people when it is empty.

Psychics have identified one of the conference room spirits as a man by the name of George. He was a lumberjack. He has also been encountered behind the lodge at a spot where they chopped wood for its many fireplaces in the lodge's early years.

In the 1970s a wing of motel rooms was built over the spot where the lodge's camping cabins once stood. Room 46 of the motel wing is reported to be especially haunted. A woman who worked at the lodge and lived in the room reported that at night objects would fly across the room. Ghosts would materialize around her bed, their faces sometimes vague and sometimes very clear. One of the ghosts was a little boy, perhaps 12 or 13 years old; another was was a man with a large knife wound across his face. She also reports that more than once she felt somebody sit on the edge of her bed and stroke her arm.

The current owners of Brookdale have been told there are forty-nine spirits in residence; they have brought in priests and psychics to try to rid the lodge of its spirits, but to no avail.

BROOKDALE LODGE

11570 HIGHWAY 9

BROOKDALE, CALIFORNIA 9500

(831) 338-6433

QUEEN MARY HOTEL
LONG BEACH, CALIFORNIA

Beaches, Sand, Sunny Days . . . but One LA Icon Puts Hauntings Afloat

Think Southern California and you think Hollywood, beaches, surf, and sun. But, southern California is also the home of one of the most haunted locations afloat: the

Queen Mary Hotel. Once a magnificent luxury ocean liner that ferried high-society dames and glamorous celebrities across the Atlantic between New York and London, the *Queen Mary* represents a bygone era.

The *Queen Mary* was built in Clydesbank, Scotland. Christened in 1934, the luxury vessel soon became known as "the Queen of the Atlantic." The Duke and the Duchess of Windsor, Winston Churchill, and many show biz celebrities including Fred Astaire, Clark Gable, Marlene Dietrich, Gloria Swanson, and Elizabeth Taylor were frequent voyagers.

After this idyllic way of life was replaced by jet travel, the *Queen Mary* was sold in 1967 to the City of Long Beach. Today, this luxury liner has been transformed into a hotel, one permanently docked at the Port of Long Beach.

Despite its tethering to the shore, the *Queen Mary*'s legacy of strange noises, moving objects, disembodied voices, and ghostly apparitions continue to haunt. It is reported that the events that occurred on board before the luxury liner was transformed into a docked hotel have given birth to the phantasmic hauntings of the Queen Mary.

During World War II, the *Queen Mary* was converted to a military ship. Painted gray and dubbed "the Grey Ghost," between 1940 and 1946, the 1,957-passenger ship carried a total of 765,429 military personnel and logged a staggering total of over 500,000 wartime miles.

Today, the *Queen Mary* sits quietly at Pier J in the Long Beach harbor. Restored to her original colors, she holds the memories of those forgotten years. And, the spirits as well. To many, it seems some of the visitors and the crew have never left.

The first-class swimming pool, no longer in use, has been

the location of many ghost sightings. The ghosts of two women who drowned there haunt it. One is dressed in 1960s clothing; the other wears vintage 1930s attire. Visitors have seen these women dive in the pool, much to their dismay because it is no longer filled with water. When someone tries to yell at them to stop, the women vanish into thin air.

Also seen in the pool is a small girl named Jackie, whose spirit still calls out for her mommy, decades after her death. The forlorn ghost of a little boy who fell overboard near the pool has also been sighted in the passageway there. Many have experienced strong negative feelings in the changing rooms at the end of the pool.

The ghost of a beautiful woman in a white flowing dress haunts the first-class lounge, known as The Queen's Salon. There are other ghost sighting areas aboard the ship. There's the infamous Door 13, where a young man named John was crushed to his death during a routine fire drill. He was only 17 and had lied about his age in order to get a job on board. In the same area of the ship, many have seen the figure of a man in overalls with a long dark beard; others say they've heard knocking from the pipes near the door and have seen bright lights with smoke in front of the door; still others have felt they were being watched by some unseen presence. In the boiler and engine room areas you may hear the voice of the former Captain Jones.

Well-known paranormal investigator Peter James hosts a "Ghost Encounters Tour" at the Queen Mary.

QUEEN MARY HOTEL
1226 QUEENS HIGHWAY
LONG BEACH, CALIFORNIA 90802
(310) 435-3511

Little Girl Ghost Captures Hearts at Hotel Colorado

The Hotel Colorado in Glenwood Springs, Colorado, a favorite retreat of Teddy Roosevelt, takes its ghost residents and stories in stride. For more than one hundred years, this National Historic Landmark has graciously opened her doors to travelers from every corner of the earth.

It's not unusual for guests to report having seen a little girl in the hallways, bouncing a red ball, even when no children were staying in the hotel. Each report of her sighting over the years describes similarities; the girl never ages, her clothing never changes. Also, some guests have reported hearing running footsteps of many people coming directly at them. Just when it seems the invisible thundering herd will run them over, the sounds suddenly disappear.

Opened in 1893, the Hotel Colorado arrived on the scene during a thrilling time in the building of America's West. With its European-fashioned spa, the resort surfaced to serve the wealthy, to house the ailing, and to offer a playground for society's elite. In addition to Teddy Roosevelt, the guests have included William Howard Taft, the Unsinkable Molly Brown, many debutantes, society's elite, movie stars, romantics, and some of Chicago's toughest gangsters.

The Hotel Colorado's originator, Walter Devereux, spared no expense in the creation of "the Grande Dame." Situated in what is now the lounge, a sheet of water twelve-feet across dropped in a waterfall a distance of twenty-five feet from the rear-wall rim to a pool beneath. Guests could sit beside the pool in the early morning and catch trout for their breakfast. The South Court, the current courtyard, also had a large pool in its center from which an electrically-lit fountain shot a jet of water 185 feet into the air, making an iridescent rainbow spray against the sunlight.

During the roaring '20s, the Hotel Colorado became an attractive playground for Chicago gangsters such as the Verain Brothers, Bert and Jack, who used the alias of Diamond Jack Alterie. Armed in gun belts, Diamond Jack Alterie wore flashy diamonds-in rings, shirt studs, watches, and belt buckles. Surrounded by bodyguards, these big spenders arrived at the Hotel Colorado via large Lincoln convertibles. Some of the ghosts seen in the hotel today are believed to be people the Chicago toughs had to take care of.

Already a fan of the state of Colorado, the president of the United States and his entourage made the Hotel Colorado their temporary home for during a three-week bear-hunting expedition in 1905. Roosevelt's first trip to Glenwood Springs had delighted him so much that he returned year after year. On a three-week trip to Colorado in January 1901, the then vice president hunted mountain lions on the Keystone Ranch near Meeker. His guide reported that he saw

Roosevelt stretch and hang over a cliff so he could shoot a wounded lion right between the eyes.

Modeled after the sixteenth-century Italian Renaissance castle Villa de Medici, Hotel Colorado's redstone walls mirror the natural beauty of the surrounding red canyons. Nestled in the heart of the Rocky Mountains, it is near world-class skiing, hiking, white-water rafting, gold-medal fishing, and swimming in the legendary Hot Springs. And, several ghost towns are nearby.

HOTEL COLORADO
526 PINE STREET
GLENWOOD SPRINGS, COLORADO 81601
(303) 623-3400

PALACE HOTEL AND CASINO,
CRIPPLE CREEK, COLORADO

From Games to Ghosts, Town's Oldest Building Has It All

The Palace Hotel and Casino is one of Cripple Creek's original gaming establishments. In operation since 1892, it was once a major attraction for the wealthy gold barons of the era. Back then, the stagecoach stopped regularly in the town square, unloading a diverse assortment of humanity.

Today, the Palace is still alive and kicking with its casino and hospitality business. It retains the lavish décor and high-roller atmosphere and the original soda fountain serves as the hotel check-in desk.

But, in addition to the traditional game tables and slot machines, the Palace has a feature all its own—a resident ghost. Kitty Chambers appears to guests and visitors with a lighted candle, seemingly floating through the halls. According to local legend, she died in the hotel nearly a century ago, but likes to continue to spread hospitality to all.

In 1896, a fire ravaged the town of Cripple Creek, which is located on the southwestern side of Pikes Peak. It burned down most of the wooden buildings, including the Palace. It was rebuilt out of brick and reopened as a hotel, which included the Palace Drug Store.

At the same time, a Dr. John Chambers and his wife, Kitty, lived and worked on the second and third floors, where he also ran his medical practice. Miss Kitty took her duties at the hotel very seriously as she offered every amenity to make her guests feel comfortable. Every day, Kitty placed candles on each table in the dining room. At sundown, she went upstairs and turned down the covers on each guest's bed. These are the activities those who have witnessed her ghost say they spot her doing to this day.

In the early 1900s, Kitty disappeared and her name disappeared from newspaper accounts. It is believed she died upstairs in the building. What's more is that when eyewitnesses to the beautiful, dark-haired ghost at the Palace are shown pictures of Miss Kitty, they are convinced her spirit roams the hotel. And in 1932, Gertrude Dial, great aunt of the singer Stevie Nicks, purchased the hotel and transformed it back into the showplace that was its legacy.

For some reason, Cripple Creek is one of the most haunted areas in this country, according to experts. These days, this well-preserved historic town has resurrected the spirit of the Old West. In addition to the Palace, security guards and guests who stay nearby at the Colorado Grande Casino have reported seeing a ghost who identifies herself as Maggie and a gentleman friend playing a slot machine after hours. The security cameras have taped Maggie. Unfortunately, the tapes have vanished, just as Maggie does when the security guards run down to the casino floor. There's also Lily, a small girl who haunts the Bennett Avenue building.

From Memorial Day to Halloween, visitors can take the Cripple Creek Ghost Walk Tour. This tour meets in the lobby of the Palace Hotel. Tour participants then walk to various haunted sites in downtown Cripple Creek.

THE PALACE HOTEL AND CASINO
172 EAST BENNETT AVENUE
CRIPPLE CREEK, COLORADO 80813
(719) 689-2992

Dukes, Duchesses, and Death:
Storyteller Reveals Decades of Decadence and Ghostly Goings-On

Linda Spitzer, "the story lady," tells tales to listeners young and old at the Biltmore Hotel, in Coral Gables, Florida. Each Thursday at 7:00 p.m., she tells stories of the old Biltmore to guests in the lobby. She spins yarns about the history, tragedies, and stories about ghosts that have been seen in the hotel.

Indeed, where ghosts are, Linda Spitzer usually follows. Neither parapsychologist nor a ghost buster, Spitzer is a storyteller of long standing who has entertained South Floridians for years. The self-described "ghost maven of Miami" founded the Miami Storytellers Guild in 1990. She is best known locally for her eight-year stint sharing spirited stories to guests, boy scout troops, and townspeople alike who are drawn to her spirited tales about the Biltmore.

Psychic Nancy Myer once studied photos of the Biltmore and discovered, by looking at a photo of the balcony, that a couple had been murdered there. She claimed they were having an affair and were shot by the wife's husband. The woman was naked except for her jewelry.

"The Biltmore was the most haunted site we ever worked on, bar none," said Dwight Sidway, a contractor involved in the renovation of the Biltmore during the 1990s, who also salvaged the haunted Geiser Grand hotel in Oregon.

To many Floridians, the Biltmore conjures up images of hotel opulence past and present. Built in 1926, the hotel's grounds not only house the largest pool in the continental United States, it contains stories of decadence and delight- but sometimes, those stories also involve death, and from those deaths, ghosts. No question the haunting happenings are directly related to the hotel's rich history.

The Biltmore made it through the nation's economic lulls in the late 1920s and 1930s by hosting aquatic galas that kept the hotel in the spotlight and drew crowds. As many as 3,000 would come on a Sunday afternoon to watch synchronized swimmers, bathing beauties, alligator wrestling and young Jackie Ott, the boy wonder who would dive from an eighty-five-foot platform into the hotel's 60,000 gallon pool. Johnny Weissmuller, prior to his tree-swinging days in Hollywood, broke the world record at the Biltmore pool, while working as a swimming instructor.

With the onset of World War II, the United States War Department converted the Biltmore into a hospital. The Biltmore remained a VA hospital until 1968, when it became the early site of the University of Miami's School of Medicine. The City of Coral Gables took over the property in 1973 and kept it vacant until the 1980s.

The Biltmore reopened as a hotel in 1994, with new

haunting episodes reported. Some of them were from the hotel's good-time days: Dancing couples in 1920s clothing have been spotted in the ballroom, and the ghost of gangster Thomas "Fats" Walsh, who ran an illicit thirteenth-floor casino back in the day, has been known to play pranks on guests.

Guests have reported opening windows before retiring, only to awaken in the middle of the night and find them shut. One guest reported a gold light shining in the corner of the ceiling and a slender figure stooping over her on the edge of the bed where she was sleeping. The slender figure was a young man in hospital gown. When the guest inquired about the strange activity the next day, she was told that during the war the hotel was a Veteran's Hospital, and the young man must have been one of the patients.

When the Biltmore reopened in the 1990s, a dishwasher who wandered into the country club building was startled to see the ghost of a man in a top hat playing the piano. But, this is not an unusual occurrence, according to the hotel's story-teller, Linda Spitzer. She had planned to focus on historical events when she first began there in 1994, but she was inundated with stories of ghosts seen by guests and employees alike. These days, she holds audiences spellbound with her ghostly tales of the Biltmore.

THE BILTMORE HOTEL
1200 ANASTASIA AVENUE
CORAL GABLES, FLORIDA 33134
(305) 913-3187

A Lady and a Gentleman: Unrequited Love, Unopened Letters, Couple Reunited in Death

Irish-born Thomas Rowe was the creative force behind Florida's Don CeSar Beach Resort & Spa. He spent three years, from 1925 to 1928, and $1.2 million, building the "Pink Palace," so dubbed for its exterior color.

But after Rowe's death in 1940, the Don CeSar fell into disrepair; it was restored to its original splendor and reopened in 1973. Since then, several guests and staffers have reported seeing Rowe, and, in some cases, being spoken to by him. He appears in the garden wearing his customary Panama hat, and light-colored suit, and walking arm in arm with the love of his life, Lucinda.

During the renovation in the 1970s, tales of Rowe's ghostly visits abounded. Construction workers and staff reported seeing Rowe's ghost, often walking on the beach or near one of the hotel's fountains with a woman dressed in vintage clothing. The woman was said to be Rowe's Spanish lover, Lucinda, a lady he was never able to marry because of her parents' objections.

The Don's colorful history began in 1928, when Rowe developed this property. But the love story started decades before. Rowe met Lucinda in the 1890s when he was studying in London. However, Lucinda's parents forbade the relationship, and the forlorn Rowe returned to the United States heartbroken. For years, his letters to his beloved were returned unopened.

When Rowe built the famous Florida fairy-tale castle, known as the Pink Palace, he intended it to stand as a tribute to is long-lost love. The lobby of the hotel included a replica of the courtyard and fountain where Rowe and Lucinda used to meet in London.

Even though their love was forbidden in life, the couple is united in death, as guests and hotel workers report sightings of the Gatsby-style attired couple walking hand-in-hand through the halls, along the beach and in the gardens. They are staring into each other's eyes and smiling, very much in love.

The sightings began right after Rowe's death in 1940. Employees working at the hotel smell his distinctive menthol cigarettes and, when they turn to look, they see a beautiful dark-haired beauty at his side.

When the hotel was being renovated in 1973, the head of the construction crew asked the hotel manager: "If you are the manager, who is the man in the white suit who oversees us?" A photographer once caught on film a man in a white suit and Panama hat whom the employees identified as Rowe.

At times, guests complain someone is knocking at their door. When they open the door there is a gentleman and a woman standing there, not saying anything. Security investigates and finds nothing. They all report it was a man in a white suit with a lady. Sightings also take place in the lobby, the kitchen, the hallways, in the gardens, and on the beach—in other words, nearly everywhere on the premises.

The name of the hotel was inspired by the tragic romance *Maritana*, an American opera written by composer William Vincent Wallace. The story is of Don Cesar, a swashbuckling soldier of fortune, and Maritana, a beautiful gypsy girl with whom he is in love. Don Jose, minister of King Charles II, also has his eye on *Maritana*, but Don Cesar exposes the wicked minister, weds Maritana, becomes governor, and lives happily ever after-an interesting outcome for the opera. But, it was not the fate for Rowe.

Ironically, it was during a performance of *Maritana* that Rowe first spotted Lucinda, who had the lead role. Love-struck, he attended every performance. He managed to speak to her, the couple fell deeply in love, and finally he proposed to her. But, her parents forbade her to see Rowe. The two lovers continued to meet in a secret garden with a fountain. It was by the fountain that they planned their great escape. He waited. But, she never showed up.

Over the years, Thomas Rowe moved back to the United States and married someone else. But, the marriage did not last; Rowe loved only his Lucinda.

Upon Lucinda's death, her family sent Thomas a note she had written years before: "Time is infinite. I wait for you by our fountain . . . to share our timeless love, our destiny is time."

Thomas Rowe died in 1940; he collapsed in the lobby of

his hotel. He wanted to leave his hotel to his employees, unfortunately, the hotel passed to his ex-wife. Shortly after, the stories surfaced about sightings of the ghosts of Rowe and his true love, Lucinda.

DON CESAR RESORT & SPA
3400 GULF BLVD.,
ST. PETE BEACH, FLORIDA 33706
(727) 360-1881

JEKYLL ISLAND CLUB HOTEL
JEKYLL ISLAND, GEORGIA

The Bellman Calling: Ghosts Continue to Serve Up Good Scares

It doesn't take much for guests' imaginations to go wild at the Jekyll Island Club Hotel in Jekyll Island, Georgia. After all, the hotel is a Victorian masterpiece steeped in history and has been beautifully restored to its former glory, conjuring up images of the former wealthy guests who stayed there. But, it's the mysterious characters who come knocking at guests' doors that have travelers buzzing about their vacations here for years after their stay.

The Jekyll Island Club opened in 1888 as a private club for millionaires. Located on a barrier island off the Georgia coast, mostly famous guests would winter in beautiful southern seclusion. Some of the regulars included powerful families such as the Rockefellers, Carnegies, Macys, Goodyears, Morgans, and Vanderbilts-people who at the time controlled as much as 20 percent of the world's wealth. Today, guests can also enjoy the atmosphere of those times, through the grand turn-of-the-century ambiance with the hotel's ninety-three original fireplaces, high ceilings, wainscoting, and breathtaking views.

But, they are not alone.

Every morning at this exclusive club, Samuel Spenser, president of the Southern Railroad Company, insisted *The Wall Street Journal* be delivered to his room. For years, it was his ritual to drink a cup of coffee while scanning the morning paper. In 1906, he was killed in a train accident. Since then, club members and hotel guests who have occupied Spenser's room, the Presidential Suite, have found copies of their newspaper disturbed, moved, or folded in their absence. Coffee cups have been mysteriously poured or "sipped on," when guests returned from the shower or a brief outing.

One guest building, Sans Souci, was originally built in 1896 for members of the hunting club. One member, J. Pierpont Morgan, liked to sit out on the porch of his third-story apartment in the early morning hours and smoke a cigar. Guests who stay in this room and rise early say they can still smell his cigar smoke.

General Lloyd Aspinwall was to be the club's first president. He died a year before the club opened. Yet, his figure has been seen strolling along the Riverfront Veranda (now the Aspinwall Room).

A common wedding and honeymoon spot, one of the ghosts appears solely to bridegrooms staying at the Jekyll Club. Many a bridegroom has inquired about the mysterious bellman that is dressed in a cap and suit reminiscent of a 1920s movie. He delivers freshly pressed suits to bridegrooms and has been seen mostly on the second floor, knocking gently on the guestroom door announcing his delivery. Other common ghost sightings include the ghost of the club's first president and that of former executives who once stayed at the Jekyll Club.

JEKYLL ISLAND CLUB HOTEL
371 RIVERVIEW DRIVE
JEKYLL ISLAND, GEORGIA 31527
(912) 635-2600
(800) 535-9547

HOTEL BAKER
ST. CHARLES, ILLINOIS

A Crying Shame: Grieving Maid Haunts Historic St. Charles, Illinois, Hotel with Her Tears

Lawrence Welk, Tommy Dorsey, Guy Lombardo, Louis Armstrong-in their day, some of the biggest names in show business-these are just some of the celebrities who have graced the stage and entertained large crowds at the famous Rainbow Room of the Hotel Baker, a resort hotel located in the far western Chicago suburb of St. Charles, Illinois.

Steeped in history, the Hotel Baker was built in 1928 on the site of old Haines Mill and celebrated its opening with a grand dinner attended by more than 300 people. The hotel began as a dream of Edward J. Baker, a native of St. Charles, who earned the honorary title of "Colonel" thanks to his excellent luck in horse racing.

In 1918, at the age of 50, Baker inherited nearly $20 million from his sister, Dellora Baker Gates, heiress to the Texaco Oil Company fortune. Using only the interest income from his inheritance, Baker commissioned local architects and craftsmen to construct his vision of an elegant resort hotel. He spared no expense to build and furnish the most luxurious small hotel in the country. Final construction costs totaled more than $1 million, and the hotel boasted the most modern conveniences of the day when it opened June 2, 1928.

During its heyday in the 1930s, '40s, and '50s, the big band music from the hotel was piped across the Fox River into the village's municipal building and could be heard throughout the downtown. During the 1950s, the Lawrence Welk Show was often broadcast live from the Rainbow Room. But behind the scenes of the lives of the rich and famous and all the glamour that brought celebrity to this Chicago suburb, a dark underworld lurked beneath. Literally, a maze of tunnels and passageways winds its way underneath the city of St. Charles, connecting just about every building downtown and along the Fox River. Today, these tunnels, although now closed to the residents of the town, continue to be the passageways for the hotel's very active ghost guest population.

During the earlier days, the local people used to be able to use the tunnels to cross the river, without having to go all the way into the town to cross at the only bridge on Main Street. Some of these tunnels go to what are now bars, restaurants, theaters, and offices; other tunnels go directly to private homes, where escaped slaves were hidden during the days of the Underground Railroad. These days, workers have seen otherworldly apparitions moving about in the town's underground hallways.

Adding to the mystery and mystique is the fact that the tunnels under the hotel were used by Chicago mobster Al Capone and his thugs to ferry stolen merchandise in and out of town via the Fox River. Deliveries of hot goods were made to the hotel via the basement. Capone's boats pulled up, unloaded their cargo, and quickly paddled off, undetected. Al Capone's gang was known to use the basement river doors for a quick getaway in case of a raid, as well as a way to have illegal contraband carted in.

All of this deep tunnel secrecy made the Hotel Baker ripe for riff-raff and hoods and has given birth to a host of modern-day ghosts who guests and employees continue to report seeing today. Present-day hotel guests hear cries of a female ghost in rooms that once housed the hotel's staff. According to legend, a chambermaid was engaged to another hotel employee who disappeared after a late-night poker game, presumed drowned in the river outside. Distraught, she cried inconsolably for days. A few weeks later, she too disappeared. The death was thought to be the work of one of Capone's associates.

Right after the hotel's restoration, employees and guests reported seeing a ghost who used to appear in the hotel's kitchen on a nightly basis. They called him "the Little Man in Red." No one knows who he was or where he came from, but at least once every day a ghost, short of stature, wearing a red tuxedo, would walk through the kitchen from one door to the other, without stopping to say anything. He acted as if he was a maitre d' or restaurant host checking on the chefs. This went on for some time, but there are no recent sightings of the little man.

"There's all kinds of bizarre things that happen, to which we just say, 'Looks like the ghost is here again,'" says Jay Perri, financial advisor for the Hotel Baker. Indeed, the spirits of earlier days still live on today at the Hotel Baker, "and quite vividly," says Perri.

During the 1970s and 1980s, the Baker Hotel was turned into a nursing home, and continued to be that until the restoration in the 1990s, when it was renovated back into a luxury hotel. There, of course, were many elderly people who died during that time. One little old lady haunts a whole floor; she's as sweet as can be and she's reported to take good care of guests. Supposedly, she makes the rounds, looking out for the guests, but then retires to her own room. Every now and again passersby outside see her sitting and looking out the window.

There's a fancy roof-top patio that was part of the hotel's

penthouse suite where another young woman met her untimely death; she either was murdered or committed suicide there. People said that every now and again they would see the same young woman walking around on the roof when the hotel was a nursing home. This area was closed off to everyone and so there really was no way for anyone to get up there without going through a series of bolted doors. Recently, employees have spotted the little old lady comforting the young woman.

The Hotel Baker was meticulously restored and lavishly renewed in 1997, creating an ambience reminiscent of its formal splendor. And due to its architectural and historical significance, the Hotel Baker is listed on the National Register of Historic Places.

HOTEL BAKER
100 WEST MAIN STREET
ST. CHARLES, ILLINOIS 60174
(630) 584-2100

Former Hotelier and Host Continues to Haunt

In the heart of Boston, along the Freedom Trail, is the world-famous Omni Parker House, the oldest continuously open hotel in the United States. Founded in 1855, it has played host to many of the rich and famous. Literary greats like Emerson, Thoreau, Hawthorne, and Longfellow met regularly in their legendary nineteenth-century Saturday Club. Baseball greats like Babe Ruth and Ted Williams, along with politicos such as Boston mayor James Michael Curley, presidents Ulysses S. Grant, Franklin Delano Roosevelt, John F. Kennedy, and Bill Clinton, all frequented the hotel.

From its kitchen it has made American culinary culture, inventing the famous Parker House roll and Boston cream pie. The Parker House has been a training ground for internationally known chefs.

The Omni Parker House is close to Boston's theater district, and it has played an important role for thespians. Many of the finest actors of the nineteenth century made the hotel their home away from home, including Charlotte Cushman, Sarah Bernhardt, Edwin Booth, and his brother John Wilkes Booth, who was seen pistol practicing nearby only eight days before the assassination of Abraham Lincoln. During the twentieth century, stage, screen, and television stars, from Joan Crawford, Judy Garland, and William ("Hopalong Cassidy") Boyd, to Adam "Batman" West, Kelsey Grammer, and David Shiner, have made the Parker House their Boston home. Today, the 551-room Omni Parker House remains one of Boston's oldest and most elegant hotels.

It's also one of the most haunted. Employees have reported that there are several ghosts that inhabit this old hotel in the heart of downtown Boston. Doors open and close by themselves, lights mysteriously turn on and off, voices have also been heard throughout the night. Several employees have quit their jobs because they have been frightened by the lost souls who haunt the hotel.

The apparitions appear to be of older times based on the attire and hairstyles of an earlier, more aristocratic era. One of the ghosts is the hotel's founder, Henry D. Parker. To understand why Parker continues to haunt the hotel today, it is important to understand the depth of his commitment to this establishment. In 1825, the 20-year-old farm boy arrived in Boston from Maine with less than one dollar in his pocket, and in immediate need of employment. His first job was as a caretaker for a horse and cow, a job that paid him eight dollars a month. Then, he became a coachman for a wealthy Watertown woman, and, after observing the finer material things, he was set on his career path.

By 1832, he had raised enough money to open a restaurant, which he called simply "Parker's." A combination of excellent food and service won over a regular clientele of businessmen, lawyers, and newspapermen. By 1854 he embarked on a larger dream—he decided to build a first-class hotel and restaurant.

Parker purchased the former Mico Mansion and razed it. In its place, Parker built an ornate, five-story, Italian-style stone and brick hotel, faced with gleaming white marble. The first and second floors featured arched windows, and marble steps led from the sidewalk to the marble foyer within. Once inside, thick carpets and fashionable horsehair divans completed an air of elegance. Above the front door, an engraved sign read simply "Parker's." Upon opening, it was recognized as one of the finest establishments of the day.

The hotel expanded again after Parker's death; in 1925, the original marble palace was torn down, and a more modern Parker House was erected–the one we know today, which was completed in 1927. One of the original wings remained open during construction, allowing the Parker House to maintain its designation as America's oldest operating hotel. The 1927 version is even more elegant than its predecessor.

The staff believes that Parker is attempting to keep things up to his high standards, monitoring activities while walking through the halls, sometimes by continually rearranging the furniture in the rooms. During recent construction work in the hotel, workers saw Parker wearing a hardhat as though inspecting the work. Certainly, Parker is continuing his lifetime quest for hospitality and is roaming the halls and the hotel restaurant to check on his guests.

OMNI PARKER HOUSE HOTEL
60 SCHOOL STREET
BOSTON, MASSACHUSETTS 02108
(617) 227-8600

GOLDFIELD HOTEL,
GOLDFIELD, NEVADA

Called a "Portal to the Other Side": Abandoned Hotel Is home to Not-So-Friendly Ghosts

Tucked away in a small Nevada town, the Goldfield Hotel has been described as one of the scariest places on earth. It has been named by psychics as one of the premier doorways to the spirit world; those in the supernatural-know claim it is one of only nine portals to the "other side."

Built in 1908 atop an abandoned gold mine, the 154-room hotel was once one of the most beautiful hotels in Nevada. Today, it is the pinnacle structure in the semi-ghost town of Goldfield, Nevada, and, it is known for its intense spirit activity. It is said to be home to several ghosts, as well as a frequent stomping ground for psychics.

The most-told story in Goldfield is about the hotel's former owner, George Winfield, and the time he got a prostitute named Elizabeth pregnant. When she started to show, he locked her in Room 109 and chained her to the radiator. After she gave birth, he threw the newborn baby down an old mine shaft in the hotel basement, and left Elizabeth chained-up in the tiny room to die. Since her death, Elizabeth's ghostly presence has been seen in the halls of the hotel, and especially in Room 109. Elizabeth's ghost even turned up on a photograph taken in the room by a reporter from Las Vegas.

Downstairs in the George Winfield Room, George's presence is said to be strongly felt. His cigar smoke hangs heavy in the air, and fresh ashes have been found in the ashtrays there. George's presence has also been detected walking near the elaborate lobby staircase. Over the years, the ghosts of a midget standing and two small children playing have been seen near the staircase. No one is sure who they are-perhaps they are former residents who stay in the place where they were most comfortable.

Psychic energy has also been detected in the hotel's Gold Room and in the Theodore Roosevelt Room on the third floor. It is reported that the ghosts in these two rooms are particularly mean-spirited, even on several occasions attacking and trying to stab visitors who came to study and explore the haunted rooms.

Despite frequent talk of reopening the former hotel as a gambling establishment, it remains closed today. There is currently no access to the public.

To understand the Goldfield Hotel, it is necessary to know

something about the town that bears its name. Goldfield lies halfway between Las Vegas and Reno on Highway 95. As the name implies, gold was discovered nearby. Eleven million dollars worth of gold was pulled from the mines in those days. Shortly after the turn of the twentieth century, Goldfield was the largest city in Nevada.

Today, the Goldfield Hotel is a crumbling carcass, in a living ghost town of fewer than 300 people. Although most of the town is abandoned, there are few mining towns that have such an array of original buildings still in good repair. Several thousand cars pass through the town every day on their way to the big cities, and occasionally a tourist stops to take pictures of the hundred-year-old buildings and rummage through the rubble.

GOLDFIELD HOTEL

PO BOX 225

GOLDFIELD, NEVADA

(THIS PROPERTY IS CLOSED OFF AND ABANDONED.)

The Beauty and the Beast: Spirit Continues to Haunt Hotel Eatery

The Lodge at Cloudcroft, a one-hundred-year-old inn, contains the Rebecca Restaurant, which was named after a ghost. The grand restaurant bears Rebecca's name, her portrait, and a delicious unsolved mystery.

The Lodge in Cloudcroft was originally constructed in 1899 by the Alamogordo and Sacramento Mountain Railway as lodging for those who came to the mountains to search for timber for railway ties. After a 1909 fire destroyed the Lodge, it was rebuilt and reopened on its current site, a more scenic location. Immediately, the resort became a successful mountain retreat, a cool spot in the mountains to get away from the heat in the Tularosa Basin.

Several dozen employees and guests at the Lodge resort have seen the apparition of a beautiful flaming redheaded woman wearing a long dress, wandering the lodge halls. Rebecca was a young maid who was murdered back in the 1930s. Rebecca's ghost is known as a flirtatious, mischievous spirit, and she likes to use the telephone, especially in Room

101, the Governor's Suite. Guests in that room sometimes receive phone calls from nowhere, and operators at the resort say that the line to Room 101 is often lit up, even when no one is staying there. Rebecca's presence is also felt in the Red Dog Saloon, where ashtrays move by themselves, and flames suddenly appear in the fireplace.

In June 2002, a psychic-medium, Michelle Whitedove, went on a tour of some of the most haunted hotels in America. The Lodge in Cloudcroft was one of her stops. Whitedove states that there is certainly strong supernatural energy coming from the Lodge. Her psychic ability enables her to connect with her "guardian angels" to give clear and accurate information about personal issues, world events, and the future. While she stayed at the Lodge, Whitedove said she was able to shed some light on the mystery of Rebecca. Although Rebecca never manifested herself, she said a faint energy was often felt, and information was channeled through her.

Rebecca immigrated to the United States from Ireland in the 1930s and got a job as a chambermaid at the Lodge. She did make a few friends, but had no family, and when she disappeared no one knew whom to contact. As a result, her death was never investigated.

According to legend, Rebecca had a lumberjack boyfriend who liked to drink and, when he did so, became mean and nasty. He felt that he owned Rebecca, but she felt that she was a free spirit-no one owned her. Because of his job the lumberjack would be away for weeks, even months at a time. Eventually, Rebecca met someone else and fell in love. When the lumberjack returned to find Rebecca's heart gone to another, he became violently jealous and left. Later he returned, forcing Rebecca to leave with him.

The legend says the lumberjack killed her and used his ax to dismember her. Even though the people at the Lodge suspected that he killed her, they found no physical body, therefore there was no investigation.

It is said that Rebecca was confused at the time of her death about where she was supposed to go, so she remained at the Lodge. Through the channeled information Whitedove learned that Rebecca has favorite spots within the Lodge, but she roams all over.

She is a curious, flirtatious and nosey ghost, said Whitedove. She likes to hang around the golf course and play practical jokes on the players there, although most of the time they don't know what is happening.

Her portraits, including a stained-glass window, are scattered throughout the Lodge property. Rebecca—actually her ghost-could be one of the most popular resident guests in Chef Tim Wilkins's dining room. A number of signature dishes featured on the menu are dedicated to Rebecca. Chef Wilkins, who claims to never have seen the ghost, must have imagined Rebecca's favorite foods when he skillfully created Prawns Rebecca-giant prawns in a spicy blend of fresh herbs, mushrooms, tomatoes in a white wine and butter sauce, served over pasta.

The grand, historic Lodge is situated near the southern-most ski area in the country, Sunset, and lays claim to one of the country's highest golf courses-a nine hole narrow and mountainous course which is played in the Scottish fashion to create a challenging eighteen-hole event.

LODGE AT CLOUDCROFT

1 CORONA PLACE

CLOUDCROFT, NEW MEXICO

(505) 682-2566

Mansions and Plantations

The Whaley House
San Diego, California

The Most Haunted House in the United States Wore Many Faces as Theater, Billiard Hall, Ballroom, and Courthouse

Located in downtown San Diego, the Whaley House has earned the title of "the most haunted house in the U.S." and is one of only two houses in the state of California certified as haunted.

Built in 1857 by Thomas Whaley on land that was once a cemetery, the house is home to dozens of ghosts.

Thomas Whaley was an extremely successful man in business and in society. His house was for a time the center of San Diego's "high society." The San Diego County Courthouse even rented the first floor from Mr. Whaley for a brief time and to use a city courtroom. Thomas had six children, and Corinne Lillian Whaley, his youngest child, lived in the house until her death at 89 in 1953.

The Whaley House over the next few years was neglected and became a candidate for demolition. In 1956, the Historical Shrine Foundation of San Diego County was formed and stepped in to save the house. Eventually, San Diego County took over The Whaley House and restored to its original splendor, making it into a historical museum. Today, it is open to the public.

The actual hauntings started being reported shortly after the house was opened to the public in 1960. Visitors, volunteers, and museum employees have reported cold spots, footsteps, strange smells, ghostly apparitions and shadows, objects moving and floating, odd noises and lights. People also talk about the feeling of being watched when they are there.

Beyond the ghosts, the Whaley House also has a unique historical value. Over the years it has housed a granary, a theater, a billiard hall, a ballroom, a courthouse, and the Hall of Records for San Diego.

Famed psychic Sybil Leek said that she sensed several spirits at the Whaley House; she is just one of the numerous experts who claim ghostly goings-on cannot be discounted here.

Author DeTraci Regula shares her experience at The Whaley House: "Over the years, while dining across the street at the Old Town Mexican Café, I became accustomed to noticing the shutters of the second-story windows open while we ate dinner, long after the house was closed for the day. On one visit to the house, I could feel the energy in several spots inside, particularly in the courtroom where I also smelled the faint scent of a cigar, supposedly Mr. Whaley's calling card."

What's interesting about the multitude of ghosts at the Whaley House is that they all have distinctive personas. Though he died in 1890, Thomas Whaley, builder of the house, is still known as the "Lord of the House." His ghost is one of the most frequent, wearing a frock coat and top hat, and is followed by the smell of cigar smoke wafting through the air. Some people say the smell is so overpowering, they have to leave the premises. And, he's usually heard laughing, a baritone laughter that resounds throughout the house.

There are also many descriptions of flowery perfume. Thomas's wife, Anna Whaley, a petite, pretty woman who had a love of music, is often seen materializing from a ball of light and floating as if dancing with soft piano music playing. Like her husband's cigar smoke, her perfume-a sweet flowery scent-often permeates the air.

Another popular Whaley House ghost is "Yankee Jim" Robinson. Yankee Jim was hanged on the property for stealing a boat. He was described as a large-framed man, very tall for his time, with unruly blond hair. He died proclaiming his innocence, and some say it is because of this perceived travesty of justice, that Yankee Jim continues to roam the halls of the Whaley House.

Thomas, Anna, and Yankee Jim are the most active ghosts in the house, but there are others, including the Whaley's dog, Dolly. Described as looking similar to a fox terrier, this dog has been observed running down the halls, brushing up against people's legs, and chasing a ghostly cat through the rose garden into the house. Phantom dog panting has also been heard on occasion. But the most common ghostly event is footsteps. Today, loud footsteps are often heard upstairs when guests are downstairs, or conversely, downstairs when guests are upstairs.

THE WHALEY HOUSE
2482 SAN DIEGO AVENUE
SAN DIEGO, CALIFORNIA 92110
(619) 298-2482

THE WINCHESTER MYSTERY HOUSE
SAN JOSE, CALIFORNIA

Stairways to Nowhere and a Maze of Mystery Make the Winchester House a Medium's Delight

It was tragedy that led Sarah Winchester to find the ghosts. Once a prominent member of elite Boston society, Sarah became distraught following the death of her only child, a daughter, and her husband, the heir to the Winchester rifle founders.

Legend has it that Sarah believed fate took her husband and child because of the bad karma caused by the family business-the manufacture of rifles instrumental in killing people-which resulted in a curse over the Winchester family.

According to the story, Sarah believed the only way to appease the spirits was to build a monument to her dead family members and keep the construction going. At age 44, she traveled alone to San Jose, California, to build what would become the seven-story Winchester Mystery House. It is a rambling, 160-room unfinished and unfurnished house. Construction would become an ongoing process for almost forty years.

Curiosities include staircases leading to nowhere and doors in the floor. History reveals that Sarah Winchester started it all, as far as the ghost sightings are concerned. She was the first to report spirits in the hall, and she rang a bell at midnight to summon the ghostly spirits, and another at 2 a.m. to bid them goodnight.

In 1903, Theodore Roosevelt, who was then president, passed through San Jose and called at the Winchester Mansion. He was turned away with the message that "the house was not open to strangers." According to servants' tales, the only guests that Sarah entertained were spectral ones.

These days, the unusual goings-on reported in the Winchester House include organ music in the Blue Room where Sarah died, a couple lingering in the corner of a bedroom, cold spots in Sarah's bedroom, and apparitions of Sarah. Perhaps one of the oddest is the smell of chicken soup coming from a long-unused kitchen.

Since Sarah Winchester's death, several psychics have reported feeling cold spots and seeing red balls of light that fade and explode. Psychic Jeanne Borgen visited in 1975

Timeline for the Winchester House

- Sarah Lockwood Pardee married William Winchester of the Winchester Repeating Arms Company in 1862.

- Their only child, a six-month-old daughter, died in 1866, and William died of tuberculosis a few years later.

- Sarah Winchester visited a Boston psychic who told her the deaths were revenge from the ghosts of those killed by Winchester rifles, and that Sarah could escape the spirits' wrath by moving west and building a house that would never be finished.

- Sarah Winchester took her $20 million cash inheritance and $1,000-a-day income and moved west to California in 1884. She bought an unfinished eight-room farmhouse near San Jose that is now known as the Winchester Mystery House.

- She soon started building on the house maniacally, 24 hours a day, seven days a week, and she never stopped. For the next 38 years, the house grew along a California highway, swallowing up everything around it including the barn and water tower.

- In the end, she created a sprawling structure covering six acres with 160 rooms, 13 bathrooms, 6 kitchens, 40 staircases, 47 fireplaces, 2,000 doors, and 10,000 windows.

and reportedly took on Sarah Winchester's appearance for a short time. Authors Richard Winer and Nancy Osborn spent the night there in 1979 while researching a book and were awakened by footsteps and piano music.

Staff members have also reported seeing apparitions and lights going on and off, hearing whispering sounds, and security alarms being triggered from inside the house. Apparitions of Sarah have also been photographed. These days the house is open for visitors of all kinds.

THE WINCHESTER MYSTERY HOUSE
525 SOUTH WINCHESTER BLVD
SAN JOSE, CALIFORNIA 95128-2588
(408) 247-2101

JANE ADDAMS'S HULL HOUSE
CHICAGO, ILLINOIS

Most Famous Social Settlement in American History Haunted by "Devil Baby"

In 1856, Charles J. Hull built the mansion as his home in what was then a fine suburban area in the southwest part of Chicago. After the Chicago Fire of 1871, many of the well-to-do moved away, and the Near West Side attracted Italian, Greek, Irish, and Jewish settlers.

In 1889, Jane Addams, a leader in the reform and women's movements, and Ellen Gates Starr started a social settlement for the poor, especially the large immigrant population in the immediate area. It became the first official welfare center in the United States.

Ghostly rumors and superstition didn't start unti 1913 when a child was brought to Hull House who supposedly had a tail and pointed ears resembling Satan-a cursed baby. There were many theories surrounding the reason for the curse. One was that the child was born to a devout Catholic woman and her atheist husband and the baby was cursed for his mother's sin of marrying outside the faith. Other rumors were that the mother had lied about a previous baby, was promiscuous, or that the father tore a picture of the Virgin Mary off the wall.

Whatever the reason, the story of the child spread like wildfire. For weeks, Hull House received hundreds of calls from visitors wanting to see "the Devil Baby."

The frenzy eventually died down, but to this day passersby report spotting the Devil Baby in the upstairs left attic window.

These days Hull House is a museum that is a popular spot on "Haunted Chicago" tours. Hull House is located on the University of Illinois Chicago campus, next to the Circle Center.

HULL HOUSE
800 S. HALSTED ST.
CHICAGO, ILLINOIS 60607
(312) 413-5353

Pirates of the Plantation: From Indigo to Buried Treasure, Destrehan Holds a Rich History of Hauntings

Built in 1787, Destrehan Plantation House, on the banks of the Mississippi River, is the oldest documented plantation in the lower Mississippi Valley. Located about 13 miles north of New Orleans, the manor home has survived colonial and civil wars and the perils of time. It carries a rich legacy both as a provider of a profitable indigo cash crop and a colorful heritage of owners who helped drive its success.

It's also home to the haunting of a former owner and an infamous local pirate who are said to appear to tourists and tour guides. Indeed, after the plantation's restoration in the 1980's, ghosts began to appear regularly to staff and tourists. The ghostly figures, phantom lights, and disembodied voices have been seen and heard and are said to be one of the former owners, Stephen Henderson, and his close friend, Jean Laffitte, a pirate who raided ships in the Gulf of Mexico. Laffitte is believed to have buried some of his treasures at Destrehan.

The original builder was Charles Paquet, who sold it to

indigo planter Robert Antointe Robin DeLogny and his family. Besides his profitable indigo cash crop, DeLogny's local claim to fame was his famous son-in-law, Jean Noel Destrehan, who married his daughter Marie-Claude in 1786. Destrehan was the son of Jean Baptiste Destrehan de Tours, royal treasurer of the French colony of Louisiana, and it is from him that both the name of the plantation and the name of the town are derived.

After DeLogny's death in 1792, the Destrehans inherited the plantation and house. While under the ownership of the Destrehan family, both the house and grounds went through considerable periods of change. In the 19th century the major cash crop at Destrehan became sugar cane, and the house went through two further phases of construction. It was here that the process of producing granulated sugar was perfected, and helped to establish sugar cane as the major crop of the area, replacing indigo.

Descendants of the family owned the property until 1910, when it was sold to the Drestrehan Planting and Manufacturing Company. An oil refinery was later built on the site but was closed in 1958. In 1972, a nonprofit restoration group purchased the plantation house and grounds, and they have been restoring and maintaining it ever since. The plantation has also gained some fame by having several scenes of the film *Interview with the Vampire* filmed there.

Since the restoration completion in the 1980's Henderson has been rumored to return to haunt the house. He lived here with his wife in the 1800's. When he died, it was discovered that he had written into his will a clause freeing his slaves and providing money and land to build a factory to manufacture clothing and shoes for blacks. The will was fought by his heirs, and was eventually nullified. Tour guides say that the white figure seen crossing the driveway, looking out windows and even sitting in a ghostly chair is Henderson. Visitors and employees also have reported orbs, soft whispering in their ears coming from disembodied voices and hearing footsteps behind them but no one appears to be there.

Today, Destrehan Plantation is open to the public.

DESTREHAN PLANTATION HOUSE
13034 RIVER ROAD
DESTREHAN, LOUISIANA 70047
(985) 764-9315

MYRTLES PLANTATION
ST. FRANCISVILLE, LOUISIANA

Murder She Wrote: Mistress Writes History as Most Notable Ghost

It's got all the makings of a made-for-TV murder mystery, or spooky Halloween storytelling: Dumped governess-turned-mistress seeks deadly revenge. Wife and children poisoned. The scary saga begins.

Welcome to Myrtles Plantation in St. Francisville, Louisiana. Called "one of America's most haunted homes," Myrtles Plantation certainly brings visitors back in time to antebellum days, and inspires some spine-tingling stories.

Located about seventy miles north of New Orleans, this more than 200-year-old plantation is today a popular bed-and-breakfast tourist destination. With its ornamental iron-work and plaster friezes, Myrtles Plantation is touted by some of the most popular consumer magazines to have the most interesting architecture in the South. It's also one of the more ghostly sites.

The Smithsonian Institution declared it the most haunted house in the United States, after sending representatives to spend several days in the house to research reported super-natural events. Certainly there is more than enough evidence to support the ghostly speculation. Myrtles Plantation is home to ten murders committed since it opened in the 1700s. And, it was built on an ancient Indian burial ground.

Spirits haunt the plantation inside and out, roaming the beautifully landscaped grounds and wandering from room to room. The most-repeated story is of the ghost of Cloe, a slave who worked as the children's governess and became the prop-erty owner's mistress. When the relationship ended, rumor has it she began eavesdropping on the family. Supposedly caught in the act, she had one ear cut off as punishment. And, her master, Judge Clark Woodruffe banished her to the fields.

However, she decided to bake a cake for Woodruffe and his family for a birthday party. Hoping to make them all a little bit sick, she threw a dash of oleander leaves into the batter.

Attempting to make them a little sick, she could then come back into the house to nurse them. The mother and the children ate the cake and became extremely ill.

But, the tale has a sad ending: the wife and her two children died. The other slaves, fearful of Judge Woodruffe's wrath, took Cloe and hanged her in the backyard. These days, the ghosts of Cloe, the two children, and the mother have all been spotted around the house. Cloe has been seen wandering through the mansion in the middle of the night. She has been seen peering into rooms at 3 a.m. Some say she is still checking on the Judge's children. Others say that they've seen the children, along with Cloe, jumping on beds, running down the halls. The sounds of mysterious footsteps creaking on the wooden staircase are also heard.

Though the Cloe story is the most popular haunting tale at Myrtle, many more people met their untimely deaths there and can be seen and heard wandering the grounds.

Legend has it that a young girl named Sara was very sick with yellow fever and the doctor had given up. The father of the girl, not wanting to give up on her, sent for a Voodoo woman to save her. The Voodoo woman said she could save her and stayed at the girl's bedside all night working her magic, but Sara died. Her father, out of his mind with grief, hanged the Voodoo woman there in Sara's room. Now, the Voodoo woman is one of the ghosts people claim to have seen in an upstairs bedroom.

Another spirit who makes himself known is William Winter, who owned the Plantation between 1860 and 1871. His spirit is said to linger because of the strange circumstances surrounding his death. He was called out to the porch one night and shot in the chest. He then staggered into the house and climbed 17 of the 20 stairs, where he died in his wife's arms. He is now heard climbing the steps, but only makes it to the seventeenth step.

Other ghostly activity noted at the plantation include the ghost of a French woman who wanders from room to room in search of something, a ghost at the grand piano who practices one chord over and over again, a portrait that changes expressions, and a young girl who only appears just before thunderstorms.

Visitors also report cameras not working, doors jammed but not locked, lights blinking on and off, the front dining room windows and walls vibrating, the feeling of a ghostly presence sitting on the edge of beds, and feeling a very cold sensation on their legs.

The Myrtles is now a bed and breakfast, and guests can stay in the rooms and experience the ghosts for themselves. Former owners had church stained-glass windows installed to keep out unfriendly spirits, and all the keyholes are covered, because it is believed ghosts enter rooms through keyholes.

MYRTLES PLANTATION
7747 U.S. HIGHWAY 61, P.O. BOX 1100,
ST. FRANCISVILLE, LOUISIANA 70775
(504) 635-6277

Neighboring Cape Towns Home to Supernatural History

Cape Elizabeth is a small town on the Maine coast, just a short distance from Portland, located on a point of land on the Atlantic Ocean.

Beckett's Castle is one of two of the most haunted houses along this part of the coast; both are now private residences. Built in 1871, Beckett's Castle is a three-story stone mansion that belonged to a publisher and avid Spiritualist named Sylvester Beckett. It is Beckett himself who is said to haunt this house, and he has apparently been here since his death in 1882. Most locals believe Mr. Beckett haunts the house in order to prove Spiritualism's theory that life goes on after death.

He usually makes his presence known by appearing in a bright blue form, generating icy cold spots, yanking the sheets and blankets off of beds, and refusing to allow a door that leads to a tower on the house to stay closed.

The other ghostly home along the Maine coast is Blaidsell House in the town of Machiasport. It is said to be the home

A passage from one of Beckett's poems, "Hester, the Bride
  of the Islands," reads:
If the soul dieth, if our years
On earth, of discord, joys, and tears,
Be all of life, then life is vain,
And Heaven's great work imperfect!
No! Death is but a second birth-
And man, immortal, oft returns.

The other ghostly home along the Maine coast is Blaidsell
House in the town of Machiasport. It is said to be the home
with one of the most witnessed ghosts in supernatural history.
The ghost first appeared in 1793 to Captain Paul Blaidsell
and his wife Lydia. The female spirit asked the Captain to
find her father, a man named David Hooper. The Captain
did as he was asked and when Hooper arrived, he identified
the ghost as his daughter. He asked her many questions about
the family, and personal ones that only his daughter would
know, and he became convinced that the spirit was really his
deceased child.

Word of the haunting quickly spread and caught the attention of a Reverend named Abraham Cummings. Convinced
the haunting was a fraud, he planned to expose it. He arrived
at the house and was stunned by what greeted him. He saw a
large rock levitate into the air and then turn into a mass of
light before changing into the shape of a woman.

Over the years, many more sightings occurred. A group of
more than fifty ghost hunters saw the ghost in the Blaidsell's

cellar, where they had gathered to hear her. The phantom passed directly through the crowd and spoke to them about moral issues. On another evening the ghost made several predictions, many of which were said to have come true.

BECKETT'S CASTLE, BLAIDSELL HOUSE
BOTH PRIVATE RESIDENCES
CAPE ELIZABETH, MAINE 04074

THE MOUNT
THE EDITH WHARTON HOUSE
LENOX, MASSACHUSETTS

Called "the Monticello of Massachusetts," the Mount Imbues the Spirit of Edith Wharton

Wharton designed and built the neo-Georgian mansion in 1902, a haven that documents the wide-ranging talents of one of the finest American novelists of the twentieth century. Wharton bought the 113-acre Lenox property and began to create an environment that would meet her needs as designer, gardener, hostess, and above all, writer. The Mount was Wharton's design laboratory where she implemented the principles articulated in her first major book, *The Decoration of Houses* (1897), which she coauthored in

1897 with Boston architect Ogden Codman Jr., a book now considered one of the seminal works of professional interior design. It clearly presents Wharton's strong views about good taste and moderation.

During an era of flamboyant house decoration, Wharton designed an airy, informal mansion with many design elements drawn from the houses of continental Europe. Wharton also collaborated with her niece, Beatrix Farrand, an acclaimed landscape architect, to design the gardens and landscaping of the Mount.

Wharton wrote her first major work, *The House of Mirth* (1905), "a novel of manners" that described the tensions between New York's "old" nineteenth-century elite society and the emerging economic power of industrialists and financiers, while at the Mount. The cold Massachusetts winters spent there inspired Wharton's 1911 *Ethan Frome*. After Wharton and her husband sold the Mount in 1911, Wharton refused to visit the house as "a stranger."

She continued to write in her new home in Europe and in 1921 was awarded the Pulitzer Prize for *The Age of Innocence*. In 1923, Wharton became the first woman to receive an honorary degree of doctorate of letters from Yale University. The Mount survived as the Foxhollow School for Girls until the 1970s and was later purchased and saved from neglect by Edith Wharton Restoration, Inc., through a grant from the National Trust for Historic Preservation. Now a National Historic Landmark, the Mount is open daily for tours.

Modern-day visitors to the Mount have heard unexplained thumps, footsteps, and girlish laughter. Apparitions have been seen both night and day. The female and male ghosts seen there are thought to be Edith Wharton and Henry James, a good friend and frequent visitor to the house.

A pony-tailed man thought to be James has been spotted in the Henry James Room, and a ghost thought to be Wharton has been spotted walking on the terrace. An unidentified man in a cloak and hood has appeared at bedsides, and the ghost of Edith's ex-husband Edward (whom she divorced in 1913) has also been reported.

THE MOUNT, EDITH WHARTON'S ESTATE AND GARDENS
2 PLUNKETT STREET
LENOX, MASSACHUSETTS 01240
(413) 637-1899

WHARTON'S THOUGHTS ON THE MOUNT

From Wharton's autobiography, *A Backward Glance* (1934):

"On a slope overlooking the dark waters and densely wooded shores of Laurel Lake we built a spacious and dignified house, to which we gave the name of my great-grandfather's place, the Mount. . . . There for over ten years I lived and gardened and wrote contentedly, and should doubtless have ended my days there had not a grave change in my husband's health made the burden of the property too heavy.

But meanwhile the Mount was to give me country cares and joys, long happy rides and drives through the wooded lanes of that loveliest region, the companionship of a few dear friends, and the freedom from trivial obligations which was necessary if I was to go on with my writing. The Mount was my first real home . . . its blessed influence still lives in me."

Ghosts, Poltergeists, and Apparitions Make McRaven House a Lively Place

Built in 1797, McRaven House in Vicksburg, Mississippi, has had a long eventful history. A vicious Civil War siege and battle took place in its backyard. And many war dead are buried on the grounds.

The city of Vicksburg is located along the mighty Mississippi River, which was known as the "spinal cord" of the Confederacy during the early years of the War Between the States. Union General Ulysses S. Grant knew that to secure a victory, the Mississippi must be under Union control. Otherwise, the enemy could transport troops and goods up and down the river at will.

Vicksburg held the key to the control of the Mississippi. Grant laid siege to the city. In July of 1863, the Federals seized control of Vicksburg, and Grant moved Colonel Wilson and Captain McPherson into the McRaven House.

Located on Harrison Street in Vicksburg, Mississippi, this predominately Greek revival mansion survived some of the heaviest fighting of the Civil War. Built in three sections, the house includes the original 1787 brick structure, a second part built in 1836 in the American Empire style, and the Greek Revival segment built in 1849. All three sections have been restored and are furnished with antique tools, furniture, and period art.

During the war, Colonel Wilson, who General U.S. Grant placed in charge of the Federal troops, and his aide, Captain McPherson, a former resident of the town, used the house as their headquarters. One night, McPherson failed to return from his usual rounds. A search was conducted, but McPherson wasn't found.

The next night, McPherson returned, but not in human form. And, since then, his mutilated-looking apparition has been returning to tell all who will listen that he was murdered by Confederate sympathizers and thrown into the river.

But he is not the only ghost at McRaven House. There have been sightings of Civil War soldiers walking around the house, and a ghostly young woman with long brown hair has been seen in the garden.

In the 1980s, an architect, appreciative of McRaven's elegance, bought the house, and it was opened for tours. But the supernatural disturbances continued. Once, when a tour guide was bringing a tour through the house one of the guests asked if the piano in the parlor worked. The guide pressed a key to find that it was silent. But, as the tour continued, the tour members heard the sound of a waltz being played on an invisible piano in the room.

Tour guides claimed that at times the disturbances got

nasty, almost demonic. One visitor had a door slammed on his hand, causing injury. Another visitor walked into the parlor and was pushed onto his knees.

While other old houses might report an occasional ghost or two, at McRaven, ghosts, poltergeists, and apparitions seem to be tripping over each other. Ghost hunters say it is one of the liveliest ghost habitats in the South.

Today McRaven House is a private residence, but the ghostly spirits continue to live there.

MCRAVEN HOUSE
1445 HARRISON ST.
VICKSBURG, MISSISSIPPI 39180

POPLAR GROVE PLANTATION
WILMINGTON, NORTH CAROLINA

Cape Fear Plantation Continues to Harvest Spooky Hauntings

Located near Wilmington, North Carolina, Poplar Grove Plantation owes its success to the peanut. Along the Cape Fear River, Poplar Grove and other plantations brought economic prosperity, and everywhere within the region thousands of farmers owe their livelihoods to corn, beans, peas, and peanuts.

Today, the 628-acre Poplar Grove Plantation continues to preserve the homestead feeling of a successful plantation, with the outbuildings and craft workshops typical of a nineteenth-century working community. The 4,284-square-foot, two-story frame manor house is listed on the National Register for Historic Homes. It was built in the Greek Revival style of architecture, and includes a low hipped roof with two pairs of corbelled interior chimneys, and a total of 12 fireplaces.

In 1849, when the original house was destroyed by fire, the estate was rebuilt by Joseph Mumford Foy and continued to serve as a prosperous plantation. At the time of the Civil War, Union armies took the house over and made it their command post and dormitory.

But it wasn't until many years later that the ghosts invaded. In 1980, after the Foy family sold the plantation and formed a foundation so it could be named a historic estate, it was opened to the public for tours. That's also the time the ghost made her debut. Known to most as "Aunt Nora," Nora Frazier Foy lived in the manor house from 1850 until she died in 1923.

Employees and visitors say Aunt Nora makes herself known regularly through a series of unexplainable events: flushing toilets, music playing, lights turning on and off, phone calls with no one on the other end, and pots and pans crashing to the floor.

But these occurrences are minor compared to one highly memorable incident when a visitor was walking to his car in the nearby parking lot and heard a noise, sounding like galloping horses. He turned, and saw a carriage led by two white horses, and at the reins were two people decked out in formal attire reminiscent of earlier times-when Poplar Grove played host to numerous balls and parties. The man jumped in his car and tried to follow the horse-drawn carriage, but it suddenly vanished out of sight. He searched for hours, but never spotted it again. He did find imprints of horses' hooves embedded in the gravel driveway.

Since then, the plantation has leveraged its ghostly goings-on by staging ghost watches, séances, and other haunting events, especially around Halloween.

POPLAR GROVE PLANTATION
10200 US HWY. 17 NORTH,
WILMINGTON, NORTH CAROLINA 28411
(910) 686-9518

THE OLD LIGHTHOUSE AND BAYNARD PLANTATION
HILTON HEAD ISLAND, SOUTH CAROLINA

Baynard Plantation's Owner Leads Phantom Procession of Ghosts

Hilton Head Island's rich history dates back thousands of years, when Paleo Indians roamed the area. The written history of the South Carolina Island began with the Spaniards in 1526, as they explored the coastal areas all the way from Key West to New England, naming it "La Florida." They found Indian settlements and evidence of agriculture. The Indians left a rich legacy of archaeological treasures still being unearthed today.

Adding to the stretches of sandy beaches, miles of golf courses, and four-star hotels, visitors to Hilton Head can not only hit the greens and soak up the sun, but leave with a spotting of the supernatural. The ghost of William Baynard, former owner of the Baynard Plantation, sometimes attracts tourist attention as he parades a procession of his former employees on a funeral procession through town to the mausoleum where his body was buried. Observers who have encountered him, say he is a not-so-friendly ghost, who often stops to look at them and sneer.

It's no wonder that his spirit is restless and continues to haunt. When Baynard died of yellow fever in 1849, he was buried in the family tomb, now known as Baynard Mausoleum, located at the Zion Cemetery. He rested there until the Civil War when Union Army soldiers who served under General William T. Sherman, were searching for family valuables and broke into his crypt. They ransacked the mausoleum looking for the treasure that was supposed to be buried with his corpse. They then removed Baynard's body, and it was never returned. From that day on, he has not rested in peace.

It is reported that Baynard lost his young bride to fever in 1830, and never recovered from his grief. So, sometimes when it storms at night, people have seen the specter of the mourning widower driving his wife's hearse, pulled by a ghostly team of four black horses. Witnesses have seen the carriage stop briefly at every plantation house along the route, long enough for Baynard to approach each gate. Baynard steps out and walks slowly to the gate. There he pauses, and a short while later returns to his carriage. Bringing up the rear of the procession is a line of loyal servants dressed in red velvet.

In addition to the ghost of Baynard, it's also believed that Baynard's former mistress, Eliza, haunts the socalled Eliza Tree, a large oak at the intersection of Matthews Drive and Marshlands Road. Eliza was hanged from this tree for poisoning Baynard's wife. Eliza's lifeless form was placed in a metal cage and suspended from the tree for all to see.

And another ghost continues to haunt the Baynard Mausoleum and the nearby Old Lighthouse. This particularly sad ghost is a young girl who died there during a hurricane in 1898. Her name is Caroline; people passing by often report hearing her crying and she sometimes materializes right before their eyes. She is usually seen during the fall hurricane season.

STONEY-BAYNARD RUINS
HILTON HEAD, SOUTH CAROLINA

The Old House: Romance and Intrigue Highlight Ghostly Pursuits at Former President's Mansion

The ancestral home of two U.S. presidents, the Edgewood Plantation Bed & Breakfast boasts a dramatic history as church, post office, telephone exchange, restaurant, nursing home, and a signal post for the Confederate Army to spy on General George McClellan's Union Army.

The 7,000-square-foot mansion, which is Gothic in style, is typical of the James River Plantations of Virginia homes built in the antebellum period. Circa 1849, it is one of several haunted plantations in the Williamsburg area. Edgewood features twelve large rooms with ten fireplaces, a kitchen collection of country primitives, and was once home to U.S. presidents William Henry Harrison and Benjamin Harrison.

The Edgewood's third floor was used during the Civil War as a lookout post for Confederate generals when they were camped at nearby Berkeley Plantation. The estate also includes the 1725 Benjamin Harris Grist Mill, which ground corn for both the Union and Confederate armies. On June 15, 1862, Confederate General J.E.B. Stuart stopped at Edgewood for coffee on his way to Richmond to warn General Robert E. Lee of the Union Army's strength.

Today the Edgewood Plantation is an opulent bed and breakfast inn that features stunning interiors, rich upholstery, lavish canopy beds, gold-gilded frames, lace and damask window treatments, and a double freestanding winding staircase.

It also has its own ghost, heard by generations of occupants. They call her "Lizzy, the friendly ghost." Lizzy Rowland lived at the plantation and was said to have waited at her window staring down the road awaiting the return of her fiancé who was away at war. In fact, she sat at the window so long that she managed to carve her name in the window glass, an etching that remains today. Before he could make it home to her, Lizzy's fiancé was killed in the Civil War. Legend has it that Lizzy died of a broken heart soon after hearing the news.

These days, her spirit is said to still wait by the window watching for her fiancé to return home. She usually makes her presence known only when the inn is full. Some guests report feeling tremendous sadness when they stay in her room.

EDGEWOOD PLANTATION BED & BREAKFAST
4800 JOHN TYLER MEMORIAL HIGHWAY
CHARLES CITY, VIRGINIA 23030
(804) 829-2962

Inns and B&B's

Moss Beach Distillery
Half Moon Bay, California

Ghost Brews Up Lots of Fun

I t's a popular out-of-the-way eatery in San Mateo County for San Francisco folk who want to escape the hustle and bustle of city living. But don't let the picturesque ocean view fool you. A visit to the Moss Beach Distillery in Half Moon Bay, California, presents its own harrowing adventures.

The place is haunted, as coastline legend suggests. The resident ghost, "the Blue Lady" has been around almost since the popular eatery's opening, when the bar/eatery was known as Frank's Place. These days, many diners, who come to marvel at the view of the Pacific Ocean from the bluffs, walk away with a chance encounter: a meeting with the beautiful lady in blue.

During Prohibition, the San Mateo Coast was an ideal spot for rum-running, bootleggers, and speakeasies. One of the most successful speakeasies of this era was Frank's Place on the cliffs at Moss Beach.

Built by Frank Torres in 1928, Frank's became a popular nightspot for silent film stars and politicians from San Francisco. The restaurant, located on the cliffs above a secluded beach, was also in the perfect location for the clandestine activities of Canadian rumrunners. Under the cover of darkness and fog, illegal whiskey was landed on the beach, dragged up a steep cliff and loaded into waiting vehicles for transport to San Francisco. Frank's Place-now called the Moss Beach Distillery-still retains its look and secluded location among the ocean coves.

And, the Blue Lady continues to carry on her legacy.

There are two stories about the origin of the Blue Lady. According to one story, this beautiful young woman and a dangerous man met by chance at the restaurant more than seventy-five years ago. Always wearing blue, she was a waitress and singer and her boyfriend was the piano player. One day a drifter came in and took a liking to the young woman. The boyfriend noticed the flirting going on and challenged the drifter to a duel. They went out on the beach with their guns raised. Unfortunately the woman ran between them to stop it just as the guns went off and she was killed. Ever since, she has haunted the bar-turned-restaurant and has become known as the "Ghost of Half-Moon Bay."

Another story says the Blue Lady was a married woman who worked at the bar as a waitress. There, she met a man who would become her lover, unbeknownst to her husband. According to this version of the story, she died in an automobile accident and returns to the Distillery to search for her lover.

No matter how her tragic ending occurred, the Blue Lady continues to haunt. Even small children say they have seen the Blue Lady. But, she not only makes appearances, there are unusual occurrences attributed to her-strange phone calls where no one is on the other end of the line; levitating checkbooks; rooms locked from the inside; and women diners losing one earring. In one three-week period, after several diners had reported losing an earring, several were found in one place later. The dates on the restaurant's computers are often tampered with, and the story of the Blue Lady has become so well known that the TV program *Unsolved Mysteries* has also documented it.

MOSS BEACH DISTILLERY

MOSS BEACH, 140 BEACH WAY

HALF-MOON BAY, CALIFORNIA

(650) 728-5595

Wedding Day Death Continues to Haunt the Halls of the Lighthouse Inn Resort

The timing was tragic. In 1930, as the young bride walked down the stairway in her wedding dress, she tripped, careened down the steps and broke her neck on the landing. Today, her beautiful vintage gown continues to elicit oohs and ahs when guests spot this bride roaming through the hallways and guestrooms, as if she is still trying to find her way to the altar. When people approach her, she disappears around a corner.

Built in 1902 as the grand summer home of steel magnate Charles S. Guthrie, the Lighthouse Inn Resort was originally called Meadow Court for the wildflowers surrounding it. Still today, it commands a breathtaking view of Long Island Sound. Noted architect William Emerson of Boston designed the mansion, while the formal grounds were conceived by renowned landscape architect Frederick Law Olmsted, who also designed Central Park. Meadow Court became a popular destination for social events and a private retreat for film stars including Bette Davis and Joan Crawford.

Through its more than 100-year history, this sad wedding day story continues to play out at the Lighthouse Inn, which has been host to East Coast power brokers, as well as Broadway and Hollywood stars since the Meadow Court Inn opened its doors in 1927.

Soon after being built, it was transformed from a private residence to an inn and was renamed the New London Harbor Light. Today, it's known as the Lighthouse Inn Resort and is a member of the Prestigious Historic Hotels of America.

In recent years, the Mediterranean style mansion underwent a $1 million renovation that brought the Lighthouse Inn back to its original splendor. A stay at the inn might well result in an encounter with this tragic ghostly bride.

THE LIGHTHOUSE INN RESORT

SIX GUTHRIE PLACE

NEW LONDON, CONNECTICUT 06320

(860) 443-8411

Dark Shadows, Flying Saucers, and Ghostly Pursuits Haunt This Artsy Florida Inn

Shadows looming in a dark corner, dishes flying off shelves, a ghost who tugs on visitor's shirtsleeves-these all draw curious tourists and ghost researchers to the DeLand Artisan Inn in DeLand, Florida. At the same time, the inn is also a hub for local artisans and others who display their works in its gallery.

Many believe the ghosts are a reminder of sadder times at the inn, including the abrupt end of a dream for the Michigan couple who came south to forge a new beginning. Arriving in Florida in 1913, Michigan residents Edward and Jeanette Barnhill had brought their vision to launch open-aired tour buses and to open a hotel for fellow snowbirds. While the hotel took years of struggle and complications to bring to life, the Barnhills used their innovations to craft tour buses by connecting two Model T Fords and established the first bus line between DeLand and nearby Daytona

Beach. The hotel finally came to fruition and opened its doors in 1927.

Sadly, Jeanette died a year later, and Edwin was declared insane in 1929. Over the years, without its original creators and their vision, the hotel deteriorated. In the 1980s, it was closed. At one point it was home to rats, pigeons, and vagrants; it was an eyesore in downtown DeLand. But, in 1996, new owners and a new vision for the hotel emerged and restoration quickly ensued. Today, the completely renovated DeLand Artisan Inn, with its arcade facade, parapets, pent roof with ceramic tiles, and stucco walls oozes Mediterranean charm. Its two art galleries feature works from local artists and from artists displayed in the National Museum of Women in the Arts.

The DeLand Artisan Inn has also become a must-stop destination for Daytona-area ghost enthusiasts. Hotel employees report feeling an unseen child tugging at their sleeves in an elevator and strange blue lights following them from room to room.

Other strange and unexplained experiences happen frequently: dishes and saucers flying off shelves, footsteps heard running down an empty third-floor corridor, sightings of a figure lurking in the shadows of the hotel basement. When employees approach the figure, he or she disappears into the basement's brick wall.

There have been investigations. A visiting psychic picked up on a male presence; other ghost investigators have said the inn is very active with ghostly activities, and photographs have been taken documenting the sightings.

While visiting DeLand, you can partake in a two-hour ghost tour of the area; as parapsychologists claim that many of the brick buildings in DeLand are haunted.

DELAND ARTISAN INN
215 S. WOODLAND BLVD.
DELAND, FLORIDA
(386) 736-3484

MASON HOUSE INN,
BENTONSPORT, IOWA

Knocking and Alarms Keep Owners and Guests Hopping from Ghostly Happenings

The Mason House Inn in historic Bentonsport, Iowa, is nestled on the banks of the beautiful Des Moines River, one of Iowa's very first settlements.

The Mason Inn was built in 1846 to serve steamboat travelers going from St. Louis to Des Moines. It was constructed by Mormon craftsmen who stayed in Bentonsport three years before making their famous trek to Utah. In 1989, the inn underwent extensive refurbishing. This included remodeling an old railroad station and connecting it to the Mason House.

Built to serve travelers 150 years ago, the hospitality continues there today: There's still a cookie jar in every room. And, the ghosts continue to haunt.

These days, Chuck and Joy Hanson own the inn. Joy has experienced the ghosts and shares this account:

Quite often, when we are in the dining room or kitchen on the first floor, we hear the floor squeaking on the second floor. It sounds like someone is up there walking around, but when we go up to see, there is no one there. One night, Chuck and I were in bed on the first floor, when we heard someone walking around in the Keeping Room, which is right outside our bedroom door. Thinking it was one of our daughters, I didn't think much of it. There was a knock at our bedroom door. I said, 'What do you want?' There was no answer. Just more walking around sounds. Finally it quit. I asked my daughters in the morning what they wanted, but both daughters said it was not them. And, there were no guests in the inn that night.

There have also been bouts with the clock alarms and the fire alarms when one by one, they go off in each room. No matter how many times the bed in Room Seven is made and smoothed, it becomes rumpled, as if someone were laying in it. Throughout the house, doors mysteriously lock and unlock, and footsteps pace around the inn.

C. F. Dedman, a local resident reported this experience of the ghost on March 31, 2004, sometime between 10 p.m. and midnight in Room Five, the Mason Suite: "I was lying on my side, and I was reading a book. It felt like someone was playing with my right shoulder. I pulled my shoulder away when I realized my shirt wasn't coming with me. It was being pulled. I turned to look over my shoulder, and there wasn't anyone there. The next morning I remember being weak and nauseous."

Although most of the ghosts at the Mason Inn are friendly, one spirit, who has been dubbed "John," is described as a petulant old lecher who smacks young ladies on the fanny and hangs around the shower like a Peeping Tom. Reportedly John died outside the Mason Inn when he accidentally hanged himself in the maple tree. He was looking for "Jane," who was hiding inside. She was a lifelong Bettonsport resident who had been sold by her father into prostitution.

The owner of the Mason Inn had felt sorry for Jane, took her in, and hid her. When John couldn't find her, he climbed the maple tree to try to look in, fell, and died.

The Hansons say his old feelings can sometimes still be felt today. One guest reported being smacked on the behind while taking a shower. Turning quickly, she found no one there. In the shower, she suddenly felt an icy cold, and then something tapped her on the back. She started screaming, and it vanished. Another young lady felt several tugs on her towel. These happenings are attributed to John.

"If one of the Mason House ghosts startles you," Joy says, "we scream at it, demanding that it stop. That seems to work."

MASON HOUSE INN

21982 HAWK DRIVE

BENTONSPORT, IOWA 52565-8260

(319) 592-3133

CAPTAIN FAIRFIELD INN
KENNEBUNKPORT, MAINE

Here Come the Bride and Groom Returning as Ghosts

Like many ghost stories, the hauntings surfaced during the restoration and renovation of the Captain Fairfield Inn in Kennebunkport, Maine.

Surrounded by towering trees, beautiful gardens, and other historic homes, the Captain Fairfield Inn overlooks Kennebunkport's River Green and offers glimpses of lively Kennebunkport harbor. It was built in 1813 as a wedding gift for Captain James Fairfield and his bride, Lois Walker, by her father, Daniel Walker. The two lived there for five years until Captain Fairfield died of pneumonia at the age of 38.

Though the nine-bedroom, two-story home, remained a private residence, it was restored in 1991 and has become a popular East Coast bed-and-breakfast retreat. The home is listed on the National Registrar of Historic Places.

It was at the time of the restoration that Captain Fairfield's ghost was spotted hovering in a dark corner of the basement. Since then, guests and the innkeepers have reported sensing Fairfield's affable presence in their rooms and believe he comes back to continue his role as unseen host of the mansion. Others believe he continues to welcome guests because he wants to make sure his legacy and story live on in history.

A sea captain, he was captured and imprisoned by the British at Dartmoor Prison during the War of 1812. Described as a good-looking, self-assured man, Captain Fairfield was the son of a ship captain and the grandson of James Fairfield, who had come to Kennebunkport from Worcester, Massachusetts, in 1725. He had numerous siblings and like his father, sailed a ship owned by Tobias Lord Jr.

According to legend, it was on a voyage shortly after his marriage that the mariner who was in the cotton trade decided to have his portrait painted at one of the first ports he visited on his trading mission. He sailed frequently to Charleston, South Carolina, New Orleans, and even to southwestern Europe, on to England, and then back to New England.

Because he was not sailing directly home, he sent the portrait to his wife on another ship, which unfortunately became lost at sea.

On November 1, 1814, he was captured by the British and transported by ship to England with more than 250 American prisoners. They remained at Dartmoor Prison until July of 1815. That's when Captain Fairfield and his family moved in to the mansion at Green and Pleasant Streets, which was situated on six acres of land. Early in 1820, he became mortally ill and died a few months later. Interestingly, his lost-at-sea portrait was found on a Swedish ship and was delivered to Kennebunkport at last. Today it is hung at the adjacent Brick

Store Museum.

When visiting the Captain Fairfield Inn, you will be welcomed not only by the innkeepers, but possibly, by the good Captain himself.

CAPTAIN FAIRFIELD INN
117 MAIN STREET
KENNEBUNKPORT, MAINE 04046
(207) 967-4454

COLONIAL INN
CONCORD, MASSACHUSETTS

Any house that has been lived in for nearly three hundred years has a long and complicated record, but when it is three houses composed of three original buildings, things are triply confusing. That's the case with the Colonial Inn in Concord, Massachusetts. Today, the three buildings fall under one billing.

But what's even more intriguing is that there's a ghost in Room 24. It is not known why the ghost is there, or what the ghost's name is.

One guest reported that she was awakened in the middle of the night by a presence in the room—a feeling that some unknown being was in the midst. She saw a grayish figure at the side of the bed, to the left, about four feet away. It was not a distinct person, but a shadowy mass in the shape of a standing figure. It remained still for a moment, then slowly floated to the foot of the bed, in front of the fireplace. After pausing a few seconds, the apparition slowly melted away.

These days, visitors come from across the country to learn about American history, and some specifically ask to stay in Room 24, hoping to experience the ghost. Some of the guests who have stayed in Room 24 are notable: Justice Sandra Day O'Connor was placed in Room 24, although hotel staff says it was unintentional. The many notable visitors to the inn include Franklin D. Roosevelt, J. P. Morgan, Diane Sawyer, Bruce Springsteen, John Wayne, Arnold Palmer, Steve Martin, and Queen Noor of Jordan (for whom the inn broke its no room service rule).

Wrapped in patriotic bunting each summer and evergreen wreaths each winter, the inn's porch looks out over Concord's center. Guests enter through a parlor furnished with gleaming antiques and check into their rooms from another era.

Concord's Colonial Inn has a long and distinguished history and is listed on the National Register of Historic Places. The original structure was built in 1716, and the property has been operating as a hotel since 1889. Situated on Concord's town common, now known as Monument Square, the Inn is surrounded by many landmarks of the nation's literary and revolutionary history.

In 1775, one of the inn's original buildings was used as a storehouse for arms and provisions. When the British came to seize and destroy the supplies, the Minutemen met them at the North Bridge on April 19th for what became the first battle of the American Revolution. The Colonial Inn commemorates the event every April with a parade on Patriots Day.

During the first half of the nineteenth century, parts of the inn were used as a general store, and it became a center of lively commerce in the town. The property was also used as a residence and in the early 1800s the Thoreau family moved in. Henry David Thoreau lived in what is now the Colonial Inn from 1835 to 1837 while he attended Harvard.

Beginning in the mid-1800s, the building was used as a boarding house and then a small hotel, named the Thoreau House after Henry's aunts, the "Thoreau Girls." By 1900, the property was given its current name–the Colonial Inn.

CONCORD'S COLONIAL INN
48 MONUMENT SQUARE
CONCORD, MASSACHUSETTS 01742
(978) 369-9200

Sister Act: Holy Haunting

Call it a sister act. The devotion of one nun who cared for the sick in the late 1800s is unfailing. Today, she continues to minister to those in her care, despite the fact that they've long since passed on to the afterlife, and, the former hospital has been transformed into an inn. Guests report seeing a kindly nun wandering the halls as if she is looking to help her patients.

The Sisters of Charity of Leavenworth, Kansas arrived in Virginia City, Montana in 1876, and, at the request of a local priest, opened a hospital for miners. They bought and renovated the old frame building that was formerly the courthouse, then standing conveniently near the Catholic Church. County patients paid $10 weekly and private patients paid $12 "with extra room." As mining activity declined, patients became fewer, and the sisters' wards grew empty. The hospital closed in 1879.

In the years since then, travelers have journeyed to Montana in search of wilderness adventures, but they have also sought to experience Virginia City's historical treasures: the rock art of the Indians, Lewis and Clark's route, Bozeman Trail traces, labor songs from Butte's industrial trenches, and homesteaders' reminiscences.

In addition to the nun who is spotted at the Bonanza Inn, there are ghosts at the next-door Bonanza House, the former residence for the nuns. The ghosts seen here are far from benign. One of the rooms at the inn had to be sealed because of all of the frightening poltergeist manifestations, and the apparition of a not-so-friendly man has appeared in one of the upstairs rooms at the Bonanza House. Disembodied footsteps, eerie feelings of discomfort, and bone-chilling cold spots plague both buildings to this day.

BONANZA INN
IDAHO STREET
VIRGINIA CITY, MONTANA
(CLOSED)

THE GROVE PARK INN RESORT & SPA
ASHEVILLE, NORTH CAROLINA

Mystery Lady in Pink Strolls the Grounds and Haunts the Inn

With majestic views of the legendary Blue Ridge Mountains providing her backdrop, the "Lady in Pink," shrouded in billowing pink smoke, is frequently seen strolling the grounds of the Grove Park Inn Resort & Spa. At times guests hear her laughter, floating through the halls of the 510-room Asheville, North Carolina, resort. Other times, she is bolder, tickling toes at night while visitors are attempting to sleep.

Her name is Alice and she hangs out in Room 545, where guests feel an unusual cold breeze in the hallway, and sometimes hear doors slamming and talking, even when there is no one inside. The room is booked solid year-round, as visitors request Alice's room, just to check it out. When the Pink Lady does wander, she strolls over to the old WLOS-TV building, located next door to the Grove Park Inn. (The TV station has moved to new offices.) She has been known to have played around with the TV equipment, when the station operated there, and at times was seen walking around the building.

The Pink Lady is one of North Carolina's most popular ghost stories. The Pink Lady is thought to have been a guest in room 545 in the early 1920s. She apparently fell over a balcony outside her room and plummeted several stories onto the Palm Court Atrium where she met her untimely demise.

In 1996, the resort investigated The Pink Lady's origins, and hired author and paranormal investigator Joshua Warren, who collected scientific data, searched through public records, and talked to people who had firsthand experiences with the Pink Lady. He found that although she's been sighted in many places around the Inn, the evidence pointed to Room 545, which is two stories above the Palm Court Atrium floor. In subsequent interviews with people who had no way of knowing the story of Room 545 or of others' experiences, many also mentioned this room. There have been quite a few investigations here, and some rather intriguing stills and video images have been captured. It is said that there is still another ghost that frequents the Grove Park Inn, but this ghost stays in the basement most of the time, with short forays to the pro shop.

Built by Edwin Wiley Grove in 1913 from granite stones mined from Sunset Mountain, the resort overlooks the beautiful mountains and the skyline of Asheville, North Carolina. The Grove Park Inn is a national landmark, designed at the turn of the century to lure all travelers, beckoning them with pure mountain air, an architectural marvel, impeccable service, and unmatched cuisine.

The Inn appears as much a part of the landscape as the trees. Inside the spacious lobby-measuring 120 feet long by 80 feet wide-guests mingle and relax in the scattered seating. Evenings usually find people reading, chatting, enjoying a drink from the Great Hall Bar, and rocking in the rocking chairs.

The inn's famous guests range from Eleanor Roosevelt to Richard Simmons. The guest registers include such names as Thomas Edison, Henry Ford, and General Dwight D. Eisenhower; eight American presidents have stayed here. Fans of F. Scott Fitzgerald will know that he spent the summer of 1936 at the inn while his wife, Zelda, stayed in Highland Hospital.

For decades, the inn has been a favorite year-round destination.

THE GROVE PARK INN RESORT & SPA

290 MACON AVE

ASHEVILLE, NORTH CAROLINA 28804

(828) 252-2711

Chilling, Thrilling Tales at the Chadwick Inn

Ask Jim Hodulik if he believes in ghosts and he'll adamantly tell you "no." But, he'll also finish the sentence, with "well, not really, " and start explaining that even though he is a disbeliever, he still can't quite discount a series of events that happened after he bought the Chadwick Inn in Maumee, Ohio, in 1985.

Changing the name to the Linck Inn, the restaurant owner continues to this day to seek out a definitive explanation for the ghostly phenomena that have shaped the history of this eatery since it was built in 1837 by Levi Beebe. (The name "Linck Inn," is meant to be pronounced the same as the name of our sixteenth president, as President Lincoln was one of the guests at the eatery).

"I really was a total skeptic," says Hodulik, who has since sold the restaurant to another restaurant proprietor. Today, that owner has put the building on the selling block and it has sat empty awaiting a new owner. "But, from the second we got in the building, the stories started surfacing and strange things began to happen. One of our waitresses had worked at the Chadwick for years and she started the buzz. But then, I must say I experienced some very strange things that I still can't say I have an answer for."

At the top of that list was the time one evening, after closing, when Hodulik himself was the last one in the building. He remembers going to great lengths to lock the building up and make sure everything was in its right place. The next morning when he returned early and was the first one in the building, he entered the ballroom to find a table pushed into the center of the room and two chairs knocked over. Two dirty glasses and a bottle of Jack Daniels were on the table. He had left the room empty with tables pushed along the walls the night before.

"It was pretty eerie, because there was no way anyone could have gotten in the building," says Hodulik. "It made me really wonder."

During the ten years that Hodulik owned the building, several ghost hunters confirmed that the historic building did indeed house its share of ghosts. Rumor has it that the building had been a bordello at some point. When Hodulik had the floors ripped up to renovate the building he says he found "thousands of bobby pins," under the floor.

"The story goes that one of the owners came home early one night and found his wife in bed with the bus boy, and he killed them both" says Hodulik. "The bus boy was found hanging in a doorway. People who report seeing the ghost say that they see a man hanging in a doorway."

As reported by the *Toledo Blade* on Tuesday, January 1, 2002: "Jim and Christine Wilson have owned The Linck

Inn, 301 River Road, since 1995. The business is closing down due to lack of profit." As reported by the *Toledo Blade* on Sunday, March 24, 2002: "The owners of the Linck Inn placed the property and its contents up for public auction, but failed to sell the building. If no one buys the property soon, they have entertained thoughts of renovating the structure and turning it into an apartment building."

When Beebe built the building, he turned it into a kind of old-time mall complete with feed store, post office, and general store. Stagecoaches stopped at it and the passengers did their shopping. It was later, in the 1930s, when it became a brothel.

"Except for the sightings of the hangings, mostly we called our ghost 'Casper,' after the friendly ghost, because most of the incidents seemed to be harmless, like the drinking of the Jack Daniels," says Hodulik. "And, it made our restaurant very popular as everyone used to come in and ask to see our ghost."

THE LINCK INN
301 RIVER ROAD
MAUMEE, OHIO 43537
(CLOSED)

Doctor Friends and Next Door Neighbors Spook Up the Town

Given the unforeseen and seemingly unexpected circumstances of life, it is easy to understand why Dr. John McLoughlin, once called "the Father of Oregon," would die a broken-spirited man. It also makes sense that he and his wife, and their good neighbors next door, would return in death to carry on their close-knit friendship, and try to recapture happier times.

Dr. McLoughlin, was a Canadian physician turned CEO of the Hudson Bay Company. He founded the town of Oregon City and in 1845, built the large two-story mansion next door to what is now the Barclay House museum, the residence of Dr. Forbes Barclay, Dr. McLoughlin's good friend.

Known as a caring and generous man, Dr. McLoughlin served as the town's mayor, investor, and doctor.

Not long after he moved into his new house, the U.S. Congress divested him of all his holdings because he was a Canadian citizen. He died on September 3, 1857, a bitter and broken man.

Some time after his death, his property was restored to his family. His daughter sold the family mansion, and it became an elegant hotel. Later it was bought by the owner of a woolen mill to house Chinese workers; in 1886, all Chinese were run out of town. A brothel then moved into this grand place. Finally it became an apartment building, which was eventually abandoned and became a place for vagrants. The McLoughlin House was saved in 1909 and moved to its present location, to be a museum. It is the oldest museum in Oregon. In the 1970s, the graves of McLoughlin and his wife were also moved to the new estate.

That was when the ghostly manifestations started. Today, the hulking ghost of Dr. McLoughlin, who was 6 feet 5 inches tall, and the ghost of his wife, Marguerite, walk through the upstairs hall and bedroom of this old mansion. In addition to sightings of McLoughlin's tall dark shadow, objects in the house seem to move by themselves, and disembodied footsteps are heard on the stairway and upstairs. The ghost of a woman, most likely Marguerite, has been reported standing by an upstairs window, and a phantom dog scampers through the first-floor halls.

Marguerite also smoked a pipe. While working in an upstairs bedroom, a staff person suddenly smelled pipe tobacco. As she went about her business, the smell followed her around as she worked. She theorized that Marguerite was following her around, making sure she did a good job, or perhaps she just wanted to watch. Other mysterious goings on include hanging objects swaying when there's no wind; a child's bed mysteriously disheveled one night; and a rocking chair rocking by itself.

At the next-door Barclay House, visitors have seen the

ghost of a redheaded little boy so real that a museum guide thought he was an intruder and summoned the police. A spectral black and white dog leaves paw prints, and a third ghost is known as "Uncle Sandy," a brother of Forbes. He usually appears in his old bedroom standing next to the bed, especially when an overnight guest is staying. Psychics also have sensed and seen the presence of Dr. Barclay himself.

These days, both the Barclay and McLoughlin houses are open to the public and are operated as adjunct facilities to the John McLoughlin Historic House.

BARCLAY HOUSE

719 CENTER STREET

OREGON CITY, OREGON

MCLOUGHLIN HOUSE

713 CENTER STREET

OREGON CITY, OREGON

(503) 656-5146

Civil Paranormal Pursuits: Farnsworth House Home to Almost Fifteen Spirits

Haunting and history buffs often come together at the eleven-room Farnsworth House Bed & Breakfast in Gettysburg, Pennsylvania.

Built in 1810 and recently restored to its original splendor, the Farnsworth House boasts fine dinning, comfortable lodgings, and a chance to see one of the most impressive collections of Civil War memorabilia.

And, with almost fifteen ghosts. Farnsworth House is said to be the most haunted place in Gettysburg; some say it is one of the most haunted places in all of the United States.

Confederate sharpshooters occupied the house during the Battle of Gettysburg. They used the attic of the house as a vantage point to fire at the Union troops on Cemetery Hill, just a few hundred yards away. It has been said that the deeds and the presence of these sharpshooters have left an indelible mark on the Farnsworth House. According to the folklore of the place, the sound of a jaw harp, a musical instrument commonly played by soldiers during the Civil

War, has been heard coming down from the attic when no
one is there.

Meet the ghosts:

- There's Mary, a Civil War-era phantom, and the
  spirit most often seen, who walks the halls at night.
  This kindhearted woman comes to those who are in
  distress and has been known to lie down in bed with
  the guests in an attempt to bring them comfort.
- Three Confederate sharpshooters at their post in
  the attic. They have been heard moving trunks
  around in the attic.
- Another Confederate soldier, singing to still his
  wounded comrade, as he carries him down the steps
  to the basement to die.
- A farmer carrying a child wrapped in a quilt.
- A midwife huddled over a woman in labor.

Ghostly phenomena also include cold spots felt throughout the Inn, white balls of energy or "auras," some of which
have been photographed. Farnsworth House has been featured on numerous television shows and investigated by various psychics.

These days, Farnsworth House welcomes guests and visitors to its walking tours. During the walking tours, tour
guides say the veils of the spirit world open just enough to
catch a glimpse of soldiers and civilians long dead, but still
reaching across the barriers of time.

Farnsworth House's authentically restored dining rooms
are accented by oil paintings of the two commanding officers

at Gettysburg, General Robert E. Lee and General George G. Meade. One can dine by candlelight among original decor or in an open-air garden alongside a beautiful spring-fed stream. This stone-lined stream provided a water source for both Confederate and Union Armies in the Battle of Gettysburg in July 1863.

FARNSWORTH HOUSE
BALTIMORE STREET
GETTYSBURG, PENNSYLVANIA
(717) 334-8838

PELICAN INN
PAWLEY'S ISLAND, SOUTH CAROLINA

The Weatherman: Call Him Hurricane Gray Man, the Ghost who stirs things Up Just Before Mother Nature Swoops In

He's the most talked about guy in Georgetown County, South Carolina. Folks call him "Gray Man." He's loyal, in love, rich, and now famous. And he's a ghost.

Perhaps the most-told ghost story in Pawley's Island, North Carolina, and especially among the guests and employees of the Pelican Inn, is the one about Gray Man. He's frequently seen walking on the beach, especially right before the onset of a hurricane. In fact, locals have embraced his ghostly image as their very own weather forecaster: When Gray Man appears, a hurricane is sure to follow.

The phenomenon is nothing new and has been a mainstay on Pawley's Island for more than one hundred years. Locals who have paid heed to Gray Man's warnings have always found their homes safe from the storms. As the legend goes, all those who see Gray Man can rest assured that their lives and property will be spared.

Even though he's the most talked about guy in town and everyone believes in the authenticity of Gray Man, there are several different stories about who he is and where he came from.

One of the legends behind the infamous Gray Man is that he is the fiancé of a young woman who had just returned to Pawley's Island, after being away for several months. He was so anxious to get back to his love, that instead of taking the safe route back to his home, he took a shortcut through the marsh. On the way, he and his horse got stuck in a patch of quicksand and both died. After his funeral the broken-hearted fiancé was walking along the beach when she saw a figure appear. It looked just like her fiancée. The figure warned her to take her family and leave the island right away. The girl and her family left the island that night. When they returned they found that Pawley's Island had been hit by a massive hurricane. They were very surprised to find that their home was not damaged by the storm.

A second legend is that Gray Man is the ghost of Plowden Charles Jeanerette Weston. Plowden was the original owner of what is now known as the Pelican Inn. Born in 1819,

Plowden was the heir to the Georgetown rice plantation dynasty-the Laurel Hill Plantation. Pelican Inn is tucked in between the ocean and a creek and was built in the mid-1800s as a home for the Westons. Plowden had been sent to school in Britain, where met the love of his life, a British girl named Emily Frances Esdaile, and they were married, despite his parent's disapproval. Plowden became very respected and important in the state legislature, before dying of tuberculosis.

Still others believe in a third legend surrounding Gray Man. A former owner of the Pelican Inn, who is reported to have seen Gray Man many times, says she believes he was someone she had seen before in a nineteenth-century photograph. She believes his spirit belongs to the male member of a couple who had inherited the Pelican Inn many years before, who were cousins of Plowden.

Whoever Gray Man is, he continues to watch over Pawley's Island and warn people of the approaching deadly hurricanes.

PELICAN INN

506 MYRTLE AVENUE

PAWLEY'S ISLAND, SOUTH CAROLINA 29585

(843) 237-2295

Even During the Civil War, Southern Hospitality Lived. Now the Spirit of the Soldiers Breaking Bread Together Lives On in Friendly Haunting.

Visitors claim it is one of those secret finds, a cozy restaurant and inn tucked into the heart of the Shenandoah Valley on Main Street in the downtown of Middletown, Virginia. With its Colonial architecture, guests say they feel surrounded by the past, that they can almost feel the presence of the soldier dining there, or stagecoaches pulling up, with the inn staff running out to help travelers carry in their suitcases.

The more than twenty rooms are filled with French armoires and Windsor chairs. Indeed, the charming Wayside Inn is replete with an early American ambiance.

It is also abundantly haunted.

Perhaps because so many young men met violent and untimely deaths during the Civil War, their scars and spirits are all that remain. Many believe that the fact that many of these men died in unfamiliar surroundings so far away from home is why their spirits cry out in pain, as if they are searching for their friends and homes.

Wayside Inn is one of the many places that gave great witness to these soldiers during the Civil War. There are many stories of ghosts who inhabit the inn. Most center around Room 23, where a little girl named Annie is said to have resided. There are also reports from guests who have seen figures of huddled soldiers in blue or gray uniforms, and guests who have heard footsteps and voices as the soldiers walk through the hall.

Formerly known as Wilkerson's Tavern, the inn opened in 1797, and was a popular stagecoach stop and relay station where people could get fresh horses. The history of the Wayside says that during the Civil War, soldiers from both sides frequently dined there and both were served.

After the Civil War, the tavern was purchased by a Jacob Larrick, and was renamed Larrick's Hotel until the early 1900s. Later another owner purchased the property, added on to it, and christened it with its present name.

In the 1950s, Leo Bernstein, a Washington, D.C. financier and antique collector, purchased the Inn and began enthusiastically restoring it to its present eighteenth-century atmosphere. Bernstein's passion for history began in the 1920s, when a grade school teacher ignited his fascination with history. It continued through the 1930s, as the young lawyer became a major force in business, banking, and civic life of the nation's capital. "In those days," he recalls, "people weren't collecting memorabilia like they are today, and you could pick up remarkable things fairly easily. It was really fun looking for them."

Mr. Bernstein's association with the Shenandoah Valley began when he bought the Inn. Later he founded the Wayside Foundation of American History and Arts, which now operates the Museum of American Presidents, the Stonewall Jackson Museum, and Crystal Caverns; which are in turn supported by the Wayside Inn, Battletown Inn, and the Strasburg Antique Emporium

The Wayside Foundation of American History and Arts is a nonprofit foundation dedicated to the preservation of our national heritage and values, through education. Its purpose is to encourage and enhance public appreciation, enjoyment, and knowledge of American history and arts.

THE WAYSIDE INN
7783 MAIN STREET
MIDDLETOWN, VIRGINIA
(540) 869-1797

SHIPWRECKED BREW PUB, RESTAURANT, AND INN
EGG HARBOR, WISCONSIN

Shipwrecked Serves Up More "Spirits" Than Just Those That Customers Drink

They call them their "vaporous visitors," and restaurant owners, waiters, guests, tourists, and longtime residents on most days keep the conversation flowing with tales of the haunted happenings at Shipwrecked Brew Pub Restaurant and Inn in downtown Egg Harbor, Wisconsin.

From the illegitimate son of Al Capone and missing federal agents, to a logger and a previous Shipwrecked Inn owner's ex-wife, the ghosts have made their mark at Shipwrecked, and have made sure the popular eatery is always bubbling with excitement.

Shipwrecked originally opened in the late 1800s. Lumber was a big commodity at this time, and with the nearby harbor, it quickly became a gathering place for lumberjacks and sailors alike who came for a brew and to swap stories. The popular inn and brew pub is located in Egg Harbor, one of the former villages, now turned popular tourist destination, that dot the 250 miles of shoreline on the narrow peninsula of Door County that juts out in to Lake Michigan just east of Green Bay. Door County has been dubbed "the Cape Cod of the Midwest."

It is no surprise that the Roaring 1920s was an era that would forever change Shipwrecked and allow its ghostly history to unfold. During that time, Door County, Wisconsin became a favorite hiding spot for Al Capone, the infamous gangster from Chicago. And, one of Capone's favorite hangouts in Door County was Shipwrecked. In fact, there are tunnels underneath this building (now closed for safety reasons) that lead to spots all over Egg Harbor, including nearby Murphy Park, which Capone used for quick getaways.

Shipwrecked has changed hands and names several times through the years. It was formerly known as the Harbor Point Inn. But it has remained a popular must-stop destination for Door County visitors.

One of the most common ghost sightings is of Jason, the purported illegitimate son of Al Capone who was found hung in Shipwrecked's attic. Both tourists and area residents have driven by the eatery in this bustling tourist town and have reported spotting a young boy sitting on the roof. Because he appears so life-like, they fear for the safety of the young boy, and they telephone to alert restaurant management. The restaurant has gotten very good at reassuring customers that the boy spirit will bring no harm to himself or others. It is believed that Jason may have been murdered because he was about to turn Capone in to the authorities.

Also related to the Capone mystique is a crying baby whose wails interrupt dining from time to time at Shipwrecked. The baby's mother was known to be one of Capone's "girls," and the baby was thought to be another illegitimate Capone heir. One day the baby disappeared. The next day the mother was gone as well.

Following the disappearance and in search of the notorious Capone, two federal agents-"revenuers" came to Egg Harbor in the 1920s to arrest Capone, only to be reported missing the next day. They were never found, and it's believed that their spirits continue to haunt the restaurant today.

There are other ghosts as well. A logger who was murdered at the Shipwrecked bar in the late 1800s also haunts the bar today, but steer clear: he sits at the bar but has a cantankerous disposition. A female traveler, decked in Victorian-era attire and carrying a carpetbag, is sighted frequently standing in the entrance of Shipwrecked, supposedly waiting for the stage-coach.

And finally, Verna Moore, the divorced wife of Murphy Moore, one of Shipwrecked's previous owners, is probably the most frequently seen ghost at Shipwrecked. She died in the 1990s in her cabin nearby and has been seen walking through the dining room, as if she is still keeping an eye on business and checking up on the functioning of the place. She's also been heard in the basement. Current owners report that one evening they heard a woman loudly talking. Thinking a customer had wandered down into the basement, the owner checked it out but found no one there. Usually when Verna is present it is because something is amiss or about to go wrong, though most witnesses say she is not to be feared and is a very kind and gentle spirit.

SHIPWRECKED BREW PUB, RESTAURANT AND INN
P.O. BOX 87
7791 EGG HARBOR RD.
EGG HARBOR, WISCONSIN 54209
(920) 868-2767

In the Shadow of Buffalo Bill, Shy Housekeeper, Favorite Nanny, and Caring Presence Continues as "Guardian of the Inn"

It was Buffalo Bill and his associates who kept the bar and dance floor rocking with nonstop whooping good times during the late nineteenth century at the Sheridan Inn in Sheridan, Wyoming.

Opened in May of 1893, William Frederick "Buffalo Bill" Cody led the grand march of first guests into the dining room at 5th and Broadway Streets. From the green rocking chairs on the front porch (still in the lobby today), he auditioned and hired his performers for his "Wild West Show." When Cody was visiting, he always sat on the third stool from the left at the bar.

With its unique architecture, the Sheridan Inn was named in *Ripley's Believe It or Not* as the "House of 69 Gables." Over the years, it has been the resting spot for many notables including President Herbert Hoover, Vice President Dawes, Thomas Dewey, Will Rogers, Mary Robert Rinehart, Bob

Hope, and Irma Bobanova, the premiere ballerina of the Russian Ballet Company. Ernest Hemingway penned the introduction to *A Farewell to Arms* while staying here.

The inn became the short-term home and community center for people who decided to move west to create a new life in the wilderness. They arrived on the railroad while their homes and ranches were being built. There were parties galore. The bar was known for its famous "Wyoming Slug," a combination of whiskey and champagne.

But, today despite the annual tribute to this Wild West swashbuckler, it is Kate Arnold, the kind and caring house-keeper who for almost sixty-five years ran the front desk and took care of the children of families who stayed there, whose ghostly presence continues to be felt almost daily.

In 1901, Catherine B. Arnold "Miss Kate," a shy 22-year-old seamstress arrived at the inn. She was the daughter of Thomas and Minnie Arnold of Rappahannock, King George County, Virginia. Her duties there quickly expanded to desk clerk, housekeeper, hostess, and sitter for the many children who stayed at the Inn. Many report she became a "symbol of love and caring."

Kate knew everyone. She loved to garden in the back of the inn and decorated the dining room tables and room night-stands with her fresh flowers. She never knew any other home except the inn.

Miss Kate died in 1968, and her last request was to have her remains cremated and buried in the wall in a room she occupied on the third floor for many years. Today, Miss Kate's room has been fully renovated by the Preceptor Tau Chapter of Beta Sigma Phi Sorority, which took on the full renovation of her room as a community project. It is said that she continues to be the guardian of the inn.

Her presence is felt almost on a daily basis, turning lights off and on, moving objects, opening and closing doors, and other activities that mysteriously happen from time to time. Those who have spent many years at the inn have grown to love Miss Kate today as did everyone those many years before.

In 1990, saved from foreclosure by the Sheridan Heritage Center Inc., a board of directors took over the inn and began renovating it with the help of numerous community volunteers; it reopened in June of 1991. There are no sleeping rooms available, but plans are under way to renovate the guest rooms and someday open twenty to twenty-five rooms for overnight stay.

Today, the Sheridan Inn has been renamed the Historic Sheridan Inn. Its unique architecture is documented by the Historic American Buildings Survey, and it was named one of seventeen National Historic Landmarks in Wyoming.

HISTORIC SHERIDAN INN
865 BROADWAY
SHERIDAN, WYOMING 82801
(307) 674-5440

PART II

Coming
Attractions

BEHIND THE SCENES OF AMERICA'S

HAUNTED PUBLIC PLACES

Raising the curtain on some of the haunted public places in towns big and small across America, this section offers selections on some of the nation's ghostliest theaters, colleges, hospitals, and churches.

Indeed, all the world's a stage, and so it is not unusual for ghosts to give performances worthy of applause in public places where they can find a captive audience or at institutions of learning, healing, or prayer, where ghosts regularly take up residence.

Along with the audience, actors, and stagehands that populate many theaters, ghosts often likewise inhabit the space, including, for example, at the Grand Opera House Barn Theatre in Dubuque, Iowa. Colleges, too, have their fair share of hauntings. Perhaps because young people are more open to experiencing the paranormal. The friendly ghost of world-famous football star George Gipp can still be found hanging out in his old room at Notre Dame University. Even television studios can be a site for hauntings. It's been said that Oprah Winfrey has a ghost that haunts behind the scenes at her Harpo Productions studio in Chicago.

Both ghost-story addicts and newcomers to the spirit phenomena will find in this chapter some of the most famous ghost tales in American history and discover that all types of places—maybe even your own school or theater-has a ghost story. Stories surrounding ghosts of everyday places abound.

For a glimpse into hauntings close to home, we've discovered that the best way to find out about them is simply to ask. Most tales are steeped in local folklore, and old-timers, historians, and those in the know, are often happy to regale listeners with their personal favorites. Libraries and historical societies in towns across America also frequently chronicle local hauntings. Often in the case of buildings such as schools, colleges, and government offices, inquiring ghost-seekers will need permission to gain access to visit. But you may be surprised at how many of the haunted locales are open to the public.

Landmarks, Buildings, Theaters, and Museums

PICKENS COUNTY COURTHOUSE
CARROLLTON, ALABAMA

Dark Shadows: Courtly Ghost Haunts as Popular Tourist Attraction

Townsfolk and tourists alike come from thousands of miles away to gather in the town square in front of the Pickens County Courthouse in Carrollton, Alabama. There, they gaze up at the attic window on the north side of the building. A large arrow has been painted on the wall, pointing to the correct pane in the garret. For a few coins, visitors can get a closer look through a telescope positioned across the street.

Many with eyebrows furrowed, some squinting, others through the telescope, scour the building for what they've been told is its ghost. The ghost appears to be a man's face staring at them from the indicated pane. And, if they stand around long enough, which most typically do, they will likely hear one of the town's residents relate a version of the "face in the window legend." The face is thought to be the recurring image of an African American man who was arrested in the town and jailed during 1870s.

It's also chronicled on the historical marker near the building, which tells a shorter version of the ghost story than that typically given by townsfolk. According to Corey Seahorn, of the East Alabama Ghost Hunters Group, who has visited Carrollton to explore the phenomenon, the ghost is indeed very real. And even when the building's keepers try to foil the appearances, it always prevails. "The face is as plain as day," says Seahorn. "They have indeed replaced the window several times and it reappears each time."

It seems that someone set fire to the Carrollton Courthouse; the locals were convinced that it was Henry Wells, a local African American. The sheriff arrested Wells and confined him to the building's attic in 1878, where he could see a lynch mob gathering outside during a thunderstorm.

Legend says that Mother Nature or God intervened when a lightning bolt struck the courthouse. But in doing so, the bolt also etched a portrait of the man in a pane of glass in the window looking out front. Wells most likely died of wounds he received in his capture, or from the lightning bolt, but died before the lynch mob could get to him.

For decades, courthouse workers attempted to clean off and erase the image. But they finally gave up. The image is still there, with the arrow pointing it out for tourists.

The rescue of the courthouse itself provides a modern

chapter to the story. By 1999, the building's paint was cracking and its roof needed substantial repairs. There was even talk of tearing down the building. Court proceedings had already moved across the street to a new building. A group of townspeople formed the Pickens County Courthouse Preservation Society to raise money for the needed repairs, and saved the building from demolition.

THE OLD PICKENS COUNTY COURTHOUSE

HIGHWAY 17

CARROLLTON, ALABAMA 35447

PASADENA PLAYHOUSE
PASADENA, CALIFORNIA

Ghostly Thespians

In the world of theater, actors, directors, and writers have been known to crave attention. Even in death there's usually drama. That's certainly the script at Pasadena Playhouse in Pasadena, California, where numerous well-known actors and actresses have honed their craft.

But it's not one of the stars who haunts the Playhouse. Legend has it that the theater's founder, Gilmor Brown, continues as "boss" at the building, haunting from his grave. Supposedly, he's sticking around to make sure everything is running smoothly. During his life, he was a stickler for detail. And his ghost seems the same way.

Brown organized the Pasadena Community Playhouse Association in 1917. A native of North Dakota, he had a diverse background in acting and theater company management, touring throughout the United States and Canada, before settling his troupe, the Gilmor Brown Players, in Pasadena in 1916. His performers played at many theaters there until 1924, when the cornerstone was set down to start construction on the new building.

During its Golden Years, the playhouse produced more than 500 new plays, including more than 20 American and more than 275 world premiers. It was a renowned school of acting as well as a legitimate theater, giving students at its College of Theatre Arts firsthand experience on the stage.

With its proximity to Hollywood, the theater drew many stars over the years including Dustin Hoffman, Gene Hackman, Sally Struthers, and Jamie Farr. In between, it was declared the "State Theatre of California" by unanimous vote of the state legislature. In the 1930s, 1940s, and 1950s it was nicknamed "Hollywood's talent factory."

In addition to Hoffman and Hackman, a surprising number of other celebrated Hollywood actors were discovered as students at this small playhouse including Nick Nolte (*Down and Out in Beverly Hills*), William Holden (*Sunset Blvd*), Robert Preston (*The Music Man*), Randolph Scott (*Western Union*), Robert Young (*Father Knows Best, Marcus Welby, M.D.*) Victor Mature (*Samson and Delilah*), Eve Arden (*Our Miss Brooks, Grease*), Dana Andrews (*Laura*), Gig Young (*They Shoot Horses, Don't They?*), Charles Bronson (*Death Wish*) and Eleanor Parker (*Scaramouche*).

When Gilmor died in 1960, the playhouse fell into decline, and the acting school closed its doors in 1969. Restoration began a decade later and in 1986, the Pasadena Playhouse once again opened its doors.

Today, Gilmor's back; his pranks are well known to actors and audience. His apparition isn't seen, but he has been known to lock doors, turn lights on and off, hide personal objects like binoculars, move scripts to another side of the theater, and stop the elevator at the third floor, where he once had his office.

PASADENA PLAYHOUSE

39 S. EL MOLINA AVENUE

PASADENA, CALIFORNIA 91101

(626) 356-7529

HASKELL HOUSE
SAN FRANCISCO, CALIFORNIA

An Officer and a Gentle Ghost

From a fur trader's home to officers' quarters, the Haskell House in San Francisco's Fort Mason area has a colorful and rich history. And, this home of Leonides Haskell, an 1850s fur trader and abolitionist, developed a reputation of being haunted.

Built in 1851, the U.S. government took over the building in 1863. The government transformed it into quarters for its officers stationed at the San Francisco military base. It is reported that Fort Mason military personnel knew the two-story white frame house at the end of Franklin Street in the Presidio as Quarters Three.

The haunting is said to go back to the time when Haskell House was a private residence. In September 1857, when U.S. Senator David Broderick was visiting his close friend and fellow abolitionist Haskell, he was killed in a gun duel with former Judge David Terry. The two disagreed strongly over slavery; Broderick was against it, Terry for it, and the two got into a dispute that ended tragically.

The argument became heated, and they decided to settle it with a duel. When the two men faced each other, Broderick's gun went off as he drew it from his holster. Terry fired back, striking the senator in the chest. Three days later, Broderick died at the Haskell home. The senator had spent the night before the duel at Haskell's house, where he paced about fretfully all night.

The house was later used by the Union Army as a residence for officers stationed at Fort Mason. Many of the officers who have lived there over the years say that they have seen and heard Broderick's ghost pacing back and forth, apparently reliving his anguish the night before the confrontation. They say they feel his presence and have heard his pacing footsteps. Some have also heard taps at the window. An Army colonel who lived in the house reported, "I feel that something or someone follows me about the house at times. I even feel that it watches me in the shower."

Today, the site of the duel is a state landmark where the positions of each of the combatants are marked. The Haskell House is now part of the Golden Gate National Recreation Area and bears a sign testifying to its role as the site of the senator's death. In the Museum of Money (run by a prominent local bank), the French pistols, which were used in the duel, are on display.

The location of Fort Mason itself makes this ghost haunting a popular tourist attraction. Located on the San Francisco waterfront between Fisherman's Wharf and the Golden Gate Bridge, Fort Mason Center offers people from every walk of life the opportunity to experience a unique urban recreational environment. It was used by the military for many years, but by 1962, Fort Mason fell into disuse and disrepair.

However Fort Mason was designated a National Historic Landmark on February 4, 1985. It has been recognized for its important role during World War II and the Korean conflict as the embarkation point for troops and supplies shipped to the Pacific.

THE HASKELL HOUSE
GOLDEN GATE NATIONAL RECREATION AREA
SAN FRANCISCO, CALIFORNIA
(415) 561-4700

Benevolent Ghost Haunts Bell Tower

Some call them "Snob Hills." There is no question the affluent Nob Hill and Russian Hill areas of San Francisco draw swarms of tourists and are always abuzz with activity. But more hauntings are reported in this area than in any other section of San Francisco.

The old cemetery there, now buried under tons of concrete , is thought to be the source of the manifestations. And, at least a few of those lost souls seem to have found a home in the San Francisco Art Institute at 800 Chestnut Street-the building constructed next to the cemetery.

Built in 1926 on the north slope of Russian Hill, the San Francisco Art Institute rests upon grounds that once held the earthly remains of San Francisco's earliest residents. The monastic tower, which is adjacent to the cemetery site, has been considered haunted for many years.

Over the years, a variety of manifestations, including eerie flickering lights and power tools mysteriously turning on and off, have been reported by students and the public. At one point, the unexplained activity seemed to have ceased, and the harmless ghost was thought to have drifted away. That is, until the bell tower was being renovated as a storage area in 1968. Then, a series of near fatal accidents were blamed on the ghost, who was rearing his head again. Some construction workers were so frightened that they quit. A séance was held that year to get to the bottom of the mystery. It was confirmed that the lost graveyard and its souls were creating the havoc.

Other reports of sightings include one by a former student who was taking a break on the tower's third level when he heard footsteps coming up the stairs. He watched in disbelief as the door opened and closed, and the invisible footsteps went past him to the observation deck. Other students, a watchman, and a janitor have also encountered apparitions climbing the stairs of the tower. Some years later, students partying in a room at the top of the tower had a similar experience.

These days, the tower is closed. The school says it's unsafe, citing seismic concerns, but others believe it is for paranormal reasons. They think it is because the ghosts of the San Francisco Art Institute don't want people in their tower.

SAN FRANCISCO ART INSTITUTE
800 CHESTNUT STREET
SAN FRANCISCO, CALIFORNIA 94133
(415) 771-7020

A Jug of Wine and Thou: Spirits Set Stage for Colonial Mansion's Ghosts

Built in the late eighteenth century, Woodburn Mansion once served as a stop on the Underground Railroad, and now serves as the executive residence of the Governor of Delaware.

It also plays host to at least three ghosts: two courtly gentleman and a little girl, all of whom seem to enjoy the finer things in afterlife such as sipping wine in the dining room, fireside chats, and playing by the pool in the garden.

Charles Hillyard, the original owner, is said to be among the ghostly guests. He has been spotted upstairs relaxing by the fireplace. A second ghost apparently has a taste for wine and has been spotted sipping his share and leaving empty wine bottles around the mansion.

A third ghost, a little redheaded girl, is seen wearing a gingham dress and playing by the reflection pool. Inasmuch as the pool is more recent, the young girl is believed to be a twentieth- century apparition.

In 1978, the then governor of Delaware, Pierre S. "Pete" du Pont IV and his family set the stage one evening to search out the legendary spirits living on the property. Du Pont and his wife, Elise, brought two of their children to the mansion to spend the weekend. They were intent on ghost busting, and they wanted to find out if the many stories they'd heard about the ghosts inhabiting the house were true. The spookiest encounter they experienced that weekend was with a portrait that hangs in the dining room. Throughout the weekend, it would periodically change positions.

Other governors have also reported sightings. Governor Charles Terry Jr. reported that an apparition of man in a white wig had been spotted helping himself to a decanter of wine in the dining room. Governor Castle invited groups of college students to investigate the premises for ghosts after some of the strange encounters, but they found no hard evidence of ghosts. Governor Tribbitt's wife, Jeanne, regularly checked the stairway for ghosts and even left wine out, but she had no results.

But, there is still no explanation for the missing vintage wines from the cellar.

GOVERNOR'S RESIDENCE (WOODBURN MANSION)

151 KING'S HIGHWAY

DOVER, DELAWARE, 19901

War Battles Continue to Haunt Area Around Farmhouse

A farmhouse built by Peter Valentine Kolb in 1863 was a large log cabin, with two fireplaces at either end; it was considered larger and more elegant than what was normal at that time in northern Georgia. However, a major Civil War battle at nearby Kennesaw Mountain was to give the farmhouse a historical significance beyond its unusual size and structure.

General William T. Sherman had 13,000 Union troops under his command, and was trying to defeat Confederate General Joe Johnson's troops who were dug in around the mountain. Despite being outnumbered, Johnson's troops held their position, costing the Union troops the loss of several thousand lives. However, General Sherman continued his march on Atlanta despite the heavy losses.

General Joe Johnson was a military leader who believed in retreat, retrenching, and delaying-he believed you could always regain ground but not lives. However, one of his officers did not agree with his tactics: his own corps commander,

John Bell Hood. Johnson had sent Hood and troops to nearby Marietta, to be held in reserve for future moves on Sherman's flank. But, Hood was eager to fight and eager to prove himself. He found himself in Marietta waiting for information and instructions. When he heard that Sherman's forces were driving the Confederates back, he decided to take action without informing Johnson of his plan to attack. He came head to head with two Union regiments at the area near Kolb Creek Farm House. Heavy fighting ensued, and Hood's men took a pounding by the Federals. Hood kept up the attack and by nightfall had driven them back to their reserve line. However this became the scene of a Civil War skirmish where 1,350 soldiers (350 Union and 1,000 Confederate) were killed on June 22, 1864. It became known as The Battle of Kolb's Farm.

Lieutenant General Joseph E. Johnson had this to say about the Battle of Kolb's farm, "Hood had his moment of glory and reclaimed his reputation as an aggressive commander, but at a cost the Confederacy could ill afford." Today, the original Kolb Creek Farmhouse has been preserved as historical home site and the area around it as an historic place.

The beautiful pastoral setting, however, made the area prime for an upscale housing development. In 1986 Kolb Ridge Court saw its first homes built. But the ghosts of the Civil War soldiers also lay claim to the land. Residents in some of the houses have reported seeing apparitions of Civil War soldiers walking through their homes, sitting on the ground, and dashing around their yards. They also report feeling cold spots and having the impression they are not alone.

The Tatum House is one of the newer houses, built atop the old homestead site. The owners say they've seen the shadowy figure of a man walk by their bathroom door. He seems to be donning Civil War soldier attire, a long waistcoat, and a hat. He walks quickly, swinging his arm-as if he has a specific destination in mind and is in a hurry to get there. He rushes downstairs, and then disappears from sight.

The owners have also experienced cold spots in the upstairs hallways and in the guestroom, along with unusual noises and inanimate objects moving. It seems likely that the soldiers who lost their lives in a horrendous small scrimmage more than one hundred years ago continue to haunt the land where it happened.

THE KOLB CREEK FARMHOUSE
KENNESAW MOUNTAIN NATIONAL BATTLEFIELD
POWDER SPRINGS ROAD
KENNESAW, GEORGIA 30144
(770) 427-4686

The Blue Man Group: A Man, a Rat, and a Ballet Dancer Bring Close Encounters of the Ghostly Kind

Sleep is not something the owners of Joyce House get a lot of. One night, a man appeared in the first-floor bedrooms bathed in a blue-lighted fog and interrupted their snoozing. The next encounter entails a large silver-gray ghost of a rat. And, then just when it seems that all is calm, a house guest encounters a female ghost with long black hair who awakens her.

When Sara Joyce purchased the Genesee, Idaho, property in 1974 as a private residence, she moved in with her daughter, Heidi, and granddaughter, Solara. She had no idea that ghostly beings lurked beneath its roof. All she knew was that the single-story brick building was built in 1880 and had been used for a variety of commercial purchases including for a time as a museum that housed rock crystals and Indian artifacts.

But, almost from the moment Sara, her daughter, and granddaughter moved in, strange things started happening.

First, it was the Blue Man, the ghost of a tall, thin elderly man bathed in an eerie blue who appeared in the doorway of Sara's bedroom and asked: "Do you see me? Do you see me?"

Also around that time Sara's son Bill began renovating the house. One day the phantom of a huge silver-gray rat appeared in the kitchen. Bill, later discovered the mummified corpse of a large rat under the floorboards when he was remodeling the kitchen. Whenever Bill visited to help renovate the building, he complained of spirits constantly interrupting his work, causing mischief and affecting his dreams. He tried to exorcise the ghosts, but they always returned.

Sara had a visiting ballet dancer from Australia who was awakened in the middle of the night by a female ghost with long black hair, who tried to get into the sleeping bag with her. The experience so affected the lady that she decided never to stay in the house again.

The Joyce House is still a private residence and is owned by Sara's daughter, Heidi Linehan.

THE JOYCE BUILDING
206 WALNUT STREET
GENESEE, IDAHO 83832

Murals, Music, Murder, and Ghosts Haunt the Halls of Chicago's Fine Arts Building

Chicago's Fine Arts Building is one of those dark, nobly old buildings that is completely invisible to the average passerby. But, when visitors raise their eyes to its marvelous details and the robust massing of this Michigan Avenue survivor, they are swept up in the visible history before them.

This quirky, dimly lit landmark is home to Chicago's oldest art colony. It's situated in the heart of the city's arts community, on Michigan Avenue across from the Art Institute and near Orchestra Hall and the Auditorium Theater Building. An example of the Windy City's late-nineteenth-century Romanesque design, it wraps around an Italianate courtyard that used to be a tearoom, and houses a "Who's Who" of the American arts. Frank Lloyd Wright, Sarah Bernhardt, Katharine Hepburn, and Mikhail Baryishnikov have all worked in this beautiful building.

Today it is one of the city's best-kept secrets, seldom visited by tourists. And though the building speaks to the few visitors who do show up, through the muffled sounds of staccato scales, violins, pianos, and the bark of drama coaches, there's one tenant in the building whose almost 120-year presence and voice still speaks loudly today. It's the ghost.

"The Ghost" is how owner Thomas Graham and other tenants commonly refer to the strange modern-day presence of an actor who they believe was murdered in the building. The actor played a starring role in *The Shadow* radio program.

Today, tenants and staff who have worked overnight say they feel his presence frequently. Windows and doors are flung open and slammed shut. Computer screens light up inexplicably. Legend has it that whenever the ghost was restless, one of the building's janitors used to build huge scarecrows out of ten-foot ladders covered with paint tarps. The scarecrows were made to ward off the ghosts.

Built for the Studebaker Carriage Company in the days before they made automobiles, the structure was designed by architect Solon S. Beman in 1885 as a showroom, with assembly floors above. Eleven years later, the building was converted to artists' and musicians' studios. The Studebaker Theater and the playhouse on the ground floor are now Sony movie theaters, but the Studebaker survived relatively in tact. Four elaborately decorated elevator cars, only one of which is currently in operation, punctuate the vaulted passage between the theaters.

Upstairs, the painful strains of beginning violin mingle with more accomplished arpeggios spilling over the transoms from individual music lessons. Wandering the halls, look for small markers identifying past residents of note. Margaret Anderson's *The Little Review* was published here, circa 1914-17, and other "little" magazines such as *Dial and Poetry* had offices in the Fine Arts, too. Architects Frank Lloyd Wright and Howard Van Doren Shaw worked here as well. Today, architects continue to enjoy the building's unique features, including the Fine Art's interior light well.

Turn-of-the-century details endure, from the graceful harp and garland motif on the exterior doors to the advice overhead in each foyer that "All passes-*art* alone endures." Terrazzo floors edged with mosaic tiles have stood up to a hundred years of shoe leather. The woodwork throughout the building is remarkable, but the carved brackets of the staircase leading from the ninth floor to the top are worth special scrutiny. On the tenth floor are some lovely murals suffering from benign neglect.

Today, the few visitors who are drawn to the building see the ghost, and from time to time, the ghostly goings-on make news headlines in Chicago-especially around Halloween.

CHICAGO FINE ARTS BUILDING
410 SOUTH MICHIGAN AVENUE
CHICAGO, ILLINOIS 60605
(312) 427-7602

Chicago's Version of the *Titanic* Continues to Haunt Throughout the City

It's been dubbed Chicago's version of the *Titanic*, and it is one of the largest tragedies in American maritime history.

But, what many don't realize about the *Eastland* disaster is that the ghosts of the 844 lives who were lost continue to make their souls known in at least two high-profile locales throughout the city: the Harpo Studios, home of *The Oprah Winfrey Show*, and the Clark Street bridge, located in a hub of popular Chicago night spots.

The tragic story began in 1915 on the banks of the Chicago River, just steps from the Clark Street Bridge. Nine thousand festive folks boarded four ships bound for Michigan. City-Western Electric was treating its employees and their families to a company picnic.

About 2,500 passengers boarded the *Eastland*, some lining her rails to enjoy the view, others dancing to an orchestra on the promenade deck. Even though the ship tilted perceptibly to her port side, the captain made the decision to cast off, but before the *Eastland* could get under way she capsized. Many passengers and crew were able to jump into the water or onto the wharf. However many were caught in or under the capsized ship and despite heroic rescue efforts—welders tried to save those trapped beneath decks by cutting holes in the sides of the ship, and police, firemen, and volunteers formed a human chain to save others-844 people died that hot July day.

Once widely known as the worst tragedy in Chicago and Great Lakes naval history, the *Eastland* disaster eventually faded from memory. The *Titanic* was commemorated in film, and the *Edmund Fitzgerald* in song, but the *Eastland* was all but forgotten.

HARPO STUDIOS
CHICAGO, ILLINOIS

Guess Who's Coming to Oprah? A Ghost

It's many a television viewer's dream: to be a guest on *The Oprah Winfrey Show*, or at least a member of the audience for one of daytime TV's most popular talk shows.

Today Harpo Studios is an icon of modern television production technology. But the building once served as a makeshift morgue for the victims of the Eastland. There, surviving family members would come forward and claim the cold, still bodies still dressed in their festive picnic finery.

Though they've yet to make it on camera or as a featured topic on *The Oprah Winfrey Show*, there's a crowd of ghosts said to haunt the studio.

When Oprah established her Harpo Studios in the Armory building in 1989, it came as no surprise that employees discovered the building was haunted. Security guards working the night shift reported crashing noises, the sounds of dozens of invisible footsteps marching across the lobby, phantom laughter, and the sounds of a woman sobbing. Others have encountered a ghost known as the "Gray Lady" seen floating down hallways in vintage dress. Harpo employees have no doubt that the *Eastland* tragedy left an indelible impression upon the building.

HARPO STUDIOS
1100 WEST WASHINGTON
CHICAGO, ILLINOIS 60607

A Bridge over Troubled Waters: Ghosts Still Haunt the Site of St. Valentine's Day Massacre

Nearby at the Clark Street Bridge, passersby report hearing chilling screams for help and they call the police on a regular basis; the police are also frequently called to report "luminous" bodies floating in the water of the Chicago River–but none are ever found.

Carl Sandburg penned a poem about the Clark Street Bridge and its mysterious allure. "Voices of broken heart . . . drops of blood . . . a lonely policeman" Sandburg understood the world of the Windy City, and specifically of Clark Street. Thus the Clark Street Bridge has become a monument to the anguished cries of passengers from that ill-fated boat excursion.

A little farther north on Clark Street, in Lincoln Park, unexplainable sights and sounds still haunt the site of the St. Valentine's Day Massacre. It is the location where, on February 14, 1929, rival gangsters dressed as Chicago police wiped out the infamous Bugs Moran gang.

Chicago is a town full of ghosts. And the rest of the state of Illinois has its fair share. Al Capone's victims were said to return in ghostly form to drive him crazy. The very active spirit of Abraham Lincoln is felt downstate in Springfield as well as in Washington, D.C., and in the White House. Certainly, murder and tragedy are woven together with mystery and misfortune in this Windy City.

CLARK STREET
CHICAGO, ILLINOIS

THE HANNAH HOUSE
INDIANAPOLIS, INDIANA

So Close to Freedom, They Lost Their Lives

Alexander Moore Hannah was a man with an enormously brave heart. Hannah was an Indiana state legislator, and he and wife lived quietly. However he took a stance against the specter of slavery. Although knowing his actions were punishable by law, Hannah took this daring stand: he turned the basement of his twenty-four room Indianapolis mansion into a station for the Underground Railroad. Escaped slaves hid at the Hannah House, and after nightfall, Hannah himself would ferry them in a wagon to the next station.

One night a lantern overturned in the basement of the house, and, unfortunately, several slaves were trapped and burned to death. Because the blaze had to be kept a secret, the bodies were not removed, but were buried in the basement.

Over the years, there were reports of unexplained occurrences. David Elder, the caretaker for the mansion in the 1960s, was working on repairs one day when he heard strange noises and experienced horrid smells coming from the basement.

In the 1970s, the O'Briens lived in Hannah House and operated an antiques store in a downstairs section; they saw an apparition of an older man with mutton chop whiskers in a black suit near the upstairs bedroom and on the stairs on numerous occasions–perhaps it was Hannah himself. They also experienced sounds of moaning from the basement; doors opening and closing on their own; pictures hanging on the walls moving or falling, and cold spots.

In the 1980s, Hannah House was used by the Indianapolis Jaycees to run Haunted House tours as fundraisers. While they decorated the house, they noticed creaking noises coming from the stairs when but no one was there. A TV crew was doing a piece on the Jaycee's Haunted House tour when the chandelier in the dining room started swinging back and forth for no apparent reason. A psychic was brought in, and said that there were definitely cold spots and the presence of spirits in the house. The stately red brick mansion is now privately owned and is not open to the public.

HISTORIC HANNAH HOUSE
3801 MADISON AVENUE
INDIANAPOLIS, INDIANA 46227
(317) 787-8486

Specters as Stars: Strange Noises, Electrical Outages, and Other Pranks at Playhouse

The Grand Opera House is the oldest theater in Dubuque, Iowa, and has a proud history–it has hosted such stars as George M. Cohan, Sarah Bernhardt, Ethel Barrymore, Lillian Russell, and Henry Fonda.

Originally built in 1889, the opera house is being restored to its former splendor, and is once again a stage for live theater and the home to a local thespian troupe: the Barn Community Theatre Company.

If it's true that every good theater has a ghost, then the Grand Opera House in Dubuque, Iowa, is no exception. Numerous ghosts have haunted the building for decades. Over the years, there have been many reports of ghostly apparitions and strange voices in the building.

In 1986 when the building was renovated into the new theater, people again reported hearing weird voices and shuffling footsteps in the deserted building. Employees blamed the unseen spirits for hiding objects, changing lighting, and playing pranks.

Theater hands are completely puzzled by bizarre electrical problems. In 1991, apparitions started appearing in the back of the theater. An employee saw two women in the auditorium who inexplicably disappeared. The theater managers later discovered that years before, in the 1920s, after the opera house had been converted to a movie theater, cleaning women had called police on several occasions to complain of strange voices in the building at night.

THE GRAND OPERA HOUSE
135 8TH STREET
DUBUQUE, IOWA 52001
(563) 588-1305

HAUNTED VEGAS
LAS VEGAS, NEVADA

It's Not Just the Las Vegas Strip That Lights Up

Most people know that there are ghost towns in old Nevada, but not every one knows that the state's largest and liveliest city, Las Vegas-famous for greed, crime, sex, and romance, would create an atmosphere for ghostly hauntings. But, it's an unusual but normal part of a casino employee's workday to encounter the friendly and sometimes unfriendly spirits that reside in the city of neon lights.

The ghost of gangster Bugsy Siegel is said to haunt the Flamingo Hilton Hotel. He was the owner of the original Flamingo. His specter is seen by many of the guests who stay in the Presidential Suite. He is most often sighted wearing his smoking jacket near the bathroom, which he helped decorate; his choice of green fixtures are still there. Mr. Ben Siegel's ghost is also known to favor sitting by the hotel's pool late at night.

The Tropicana has its weird history of the Tiki Mask greeter. Guests at the hotel have been greeted by a man in a large purple tiki mask. Some have had their photos taken with him, but when they are developed, the mask appears as a strange hazy purple cloud.

Has Elvis left the building? The ghost of Elvis Presley, in his white sequined jumpsuit, has been spotted by stagehands and Wayne Newton himself at the Las Vegas Hilton, once the International Hotel, where the King had made a comeback in 1969.

The Bally's Hotel and Casino is now located on the site of the old MGM Hotel where a terrible fire killed 84 people in 1980. Employees and guests have seen glowing orbs and apparitions in the halls.

The Luxor Hotel, with its pyramid design has had its share of unfortunate incidents. Two construction workers died during the construction, and others were injured. Some believe that the secret properties of a pyramid shape do not belong on the strip.

There is the sense that the Excaliber is haunted, but by whom we do not know. Customers have said that they feel they are not alone on the elevators, even when they are.

Bathroom spirits seem to favor haunting Caesar's Palace and the Mirage. In both of these hotels, sensory faucets go off and on when nobody is there.

HISTORIC RICHMOND TOWN
STATEN ISLAND, NEW YORK

Spirits Haunt Historic Neighborhood for More Than One Hundred Years

Although Staten Island is one of the boroughs of New York City, for most of its history, it has been a rural community, where farming and local tradesmen lived, worked, and thrived. And Richmond Town was a hub of the local activity.

There are many historic buildings in Richmond Town, and you can take a very informative daytime tour. Included in the tour of the historic structures and houses are the Historic Museum; the Third County Courthouse; and Voorlezer's House, a National Landmark building (ca. 1695) that is the oldest schoolhouse in New York.

Voorlezer's House is also haunted; many photographers

have noted that pictures taken around the building have numerous orbs in them.

It is the same for the old courthouse–it has an orb that lingers around the witness stand inside the courthouse. The small graveyard next to the old courthouse has many a restless spirit. The most often seen one is a young girl, anxiously looking for a lost love, sometimes mistaking living young men for him. She will approach the young men only to fade away quickly when she realizes they are not her one true love.

There are also other haunted places on Staten Island: Fort Wadsworth, where soldier ghosts play games with visitors; Wolf Pond Park, the site of the murder of several children in the late 1970s, apparently the deeds of a serial murderer who was never caught; and St Augustine's Monastery, where the spirit of a monk who went insane and murdered everyone present now roams the halls. Researchers say his presence is particularly strong in the sublevels.

These are just a few of the many haunted spots on Staten Island, known for being so close but so far from Manhattan.

HISTORIC RICHMOND TOWN

441 CLARKE AVENUE

STATEN ISLAND, NEW YORK 10306

(718) 351-1611

Raising the Curtain on Ohio as Haunted Theater Capital of America

Ohio, known as the Buckeye State, has several of the most haunted theaters in America.

Indeed, more than a few theaters in Ohio are ghost-infested.

During the renovation of the Music Hall in Cincinnati in the 1980s, it was discovered the theater had been built on a pauper's cemetery, which helped to explain the abnormal amount of paranormal activity there.

At the Akron Civic Theatre, patrons know that if the house-ghost starts acting up, it's Fred, the former longtime custodian returning to frighten away would-be vandals.

Dayton, Ohio, boasts two ghost-infested theaters, both of them said to be haunted by former staff members, who didn't realize that when they died their act was over.

There have been reports for decades of ghosts at Memorial Hall, home of the Dayton Philharmonic. It was built in 1909 and renovated in 1956. The ghost of a former custodian who accidentally fell into the orchestra pit and broke his hip more than thirty years ago haunts the theater. He died shortly after his fall, and around that time, strange events began interrupting show times: lights flickering and turning on and off erratically; footsteps heard overhead on empty catwalks.

At the nearby Victoria Theatre, which has been recently restored to its former ornate self, the theater contains the spirit of an actress who mysteriously disappeared a century ago. During a performance, she left the stage for just one minute and never returned. Her ghostly appearance and the strong smell of her rose perfume sometimes haunt the theater.

Today the Victoria Theatre in Dayton has the distinction of having more subscriptions than any other theater in the state of Ohio. It first opened as the Turner Opera House on New Years Day of 1866. Three years later, the opera house burned to the ground—with the exception of its front façade. When the building was rebuilt, the front façade was incorporated into the new building, and the name was changed to the Music Hall. In fact the theater has had a few names before its present inception as the Victoria Theatre.

So remember when you go to the theater, you may find yourself distracted by unexpected guests and unexplained actions that are not part of the evening's presentation.

VICTORIA THEATRE
138 MAIN STREET
DAYTON, OHIO 45402
(937) 228- 3630
MEMORIAL HALL
125 E. FIRST STREET
DAYTON, OHIO 45402
(937) 224-9000

Monk-eying Around

It started with a statue. A seventeenth-century German wood carving of a monk stands next to the stairway at Belcourt Castle in Newport, Rhode Island. But, it is reported that this is no ordinary woodcarving. More than one visitor has reported seeing a lifelike monk stepping away from the statue. The monk has been seen walking through the rooms of the castle, but never too far from the wooden statue that bears the same form.

The ghost of an unidentified woman has also been spotted roaming the grounds; it is believed that she is the Duchess of Cleveland, who once rented the property.

In the Gothic Ballroom, where many a ball occurred, there are two haunted chairs, each with their own spirit. Both chairs have cold spots, and if you try to sit in them, they might push you out.

There is also a suit of armor in the ballroom whose owner supposedly died with a spear through his eye. In the month of March, which is when he died, crying is heard coming from the armor suit.

Belcourt Castle was built to be the summer residence for Oliver Hazard Perry Belmont and his wife, the former Mrs. William K. Vanderbilt, whom he married her in 1895, after she divorced Vanderbilt. Mr. William K. Vanderbilt was Mr. Belmont's best friend and business partner. The divorce caused quite a scandal among the Newport social elite.

Today, Belcourt Castle is a noted Newport tourist attraction, not only for its splendid architecture and history but for the ghosts who are also part of the appeal. The current owner of Belcourt Castle is the Tinney family, whose vast art collection includes antiques and treasures from thirty-three countries. They believe that it is the antiques that are haunted. "I don't think the house itself is haunted," says Harle Tinney. "Our ghosts came along with some of the antiques."

BELCOURT CASTLE

657 BELLEVUE AVENUE

NEWPORT, RHODE ISLAND 02840

(401) 849- 1566

A Lady in Waiting: Seattle's Leading Lady Continues to Take Center Stage

The building in which the Harvard Exit Theater resides was originally constructed for the Woman's Century Club in 1925. The club, whose members were dedicated to getting the right to vote and equality for women, continues to hold meetings in the lobby. The Harvard Exit Theater opened as a movie theater in 1968, and was run by people described as eccentric film buffs. The Landmark Theater chain took over the operations in 1979, and put in another screen on the third floor. Today, the Harvard Exit Theater specializes in art films, and is the sight of film festivals, such as the Seattle International Film Festival.

Today, the Women's Century Club meets at the theater twice a week. And legend has it, its founding members have yet to miss a meeting—at least in spirit, anyway. According to reports, the female ghosts have the want-to-be-seen attitude, appearing regularly at the theater house, which is located in the Capitol Hill section of downtown Seattle.

Indeed, since the 1970s the ghost of several women

decked out in turn-of-the-century garb have been appearing regularly at the theater. The most frequent spirits include two different female ghosts who have been seen in the first-floor lobby in person and even in photos taken of the supposedly empty room. One spirit is believed to be Bertha Landis, a strong spirit in life who was the founder of the Women's Century Club, the City Federation of Women's Clubs, and was also Seattle's first mayor. The Spirit of Bertha Landis is the most common apparition spotted by the living. She seems to like to keep an eye on the place, help out the managers, and she doesn't plan to leave anytime soon.

The fact that these spirits still enjoy the ambiance and atmosphere of the Harvard Exit Theater has been the topic of many newspapers and television shows, and has drawn many psychics to investigate the building with their equipment, medium contacts, and personal experiences.

Ghostly film enthusiasts have been known to reorganize the film canisters around the projection room, much to the annoyance of the living. On several occasions, theater managers have opened the building and found the projector showing a film to an unseen audience. In one instance, a projectionist arrived and found a movie playing to an empty, dark house. He made haste to the projection room to catch the guilty party, but the door was locked from the inside.

From its inception, Harvard Exit Theater has been described as an unusual, luxurious home, more than it's a theater. The first floor main lobby is described as being grand and glorious, full of the 1920s ambiance, featuring a grand piano and a beautiful chandelier. Comfortable chairs, some with tables and lamps, are grouped around the huge fireplace, which is always traditionally lit for the patrons.

HARVARD EXIT THEATER

807 ROY STREET

SEATTLE, WASHINGTON 98102

(206) 323-8985

Schools, Libraries, and Hospitals

Harding University
Searcy, Arkansas

The Pianist Ghost

A pianist's music can sometimes be haunting. But, for those who head up U.S. Highway 67 to Searcy, Arkansas, to see Harding University and the ghost that haunts its hallowed halls, they may be surprised by the ghostly magic from the old music building.

Legend has it that in the 1930s a young woman with a promising music career attended Galloway Women's College, which was housed on the same grounds as present-day Harding University. She met and immediately fell madly in love with a young man, but before their relationship could fully bloom he was killed in a car accident. She was grief stricken because of this tragedy and fell into a deep depression. Her fellow students would hear her playing the piano on the third floor of the music building every waking hour of the day.

Shortly after, she too died—no one was quite sure of the cause but a broken heart must have played into it. Students reported still hearing piano music emanating from the third floor of the music building. When they investigated, they would find no one at the piano. Many believed it was the tragic young woman playing for her lost love.

The old building was torn down and replaced with a modern two story building. However, students report that they still hear piano music coming from what would be the third story.

Galloway Women's College merged with Hendrix College in 1933 in Conway, Arkansas; Harding College bought the old Galloway campus and buildings; students still say they hear piano music gently playing late at night.

HARDING UNIVERSITY

900 EAST CENTER STREET

SEARCY, ARKANSAS 72149

Anguish and Despair Continue to Haunt Playground and Former Site of State Hospital

Today, it is a playground, with swings and slides, and children running, laughing, and playing. But the ghosts of sadder times still haunt the 130-acres located near Silver and Hiawassee Roads in Orlando Florida. Ghost busters and psychics say the property continues to hold the despair, anguish, and guilt that once shrouded the Sunnyland Hospital before the building was torn down in 1999.

The hospital was opened in the 1940s as a treatment facility for tuberculosis. Later it became a mental hospital; the hospital closed its doors in 1985 after a class-action suit alleging patient neglect and poor treatment. Conditions in this three-story building when it was a hospital were said to be nightmarish.

Many traveled to the former hospital before it was torn down to catch a glimpse of the ghosts that were said to be there and to share ghostly stories. There were many reports of flashes of light emanating from the third floor, and the sound of things being dropped, or thrown, from the windows.

Sometimes, curious explorers braved the no trespassing signs and entered the darkened abandoned building. On one occasion, two people roaming the third level were met by two ghostly residents. The first ghost was the spirit of a young boy. He was observed on the hospital's upper level, ducking from doorway to doorway, seemingly looking for someone or something. The young ghost briefly paused and stared at the visitors, but then resumed his endless quest. The second apparition was that of a terrified young girl found screaming on the landing of the third-floor stairs. It is said that when she saw the trespassers, she threw herself off the third-floor landing. But no body was found below.

Since the building was torn down in the late 1990s, investigators from the Central Florida Ghost Society have visited the site and reported the presence of strong energy fluctuations around the former hospital site and the parking lot; some have captured images of anomalies (called orbs) that suggest spirit activity.

The demolition of the hospital and the building of a playground has apparently not stopped the spirits from returning to the site of despair once known as Sunnyland Hospital.

SUNNYLAND HOSPITAL (NOW A PLAYGROUND)

INTERSECTION OF SILVER AND HIAWASSEE ROADS

ORLANDO, FLORIDA 32808

Old School: Kids and Skateboarding Ghost Continue to Haunt Dorm Halls

Talk about location, location, location. For ghosts who want to keep their spirits in this world, no one can argue that Chaminade University in Honolulu is not a prime spot to stick around and haunt. Located on the slopes of Kalaepohaku in suburban Honolulu, two miles from Waikiki Beach, this small Catholic university is said to be the home for several ghosts.

One looks and behaves like any sophomore on campus, making his spirit and presence known by skateboarding around the dorms. The sophomore ghost, who is usually seen around Halloween-his favorite holiday-is said to be the spirit of a sophomore who was killed in a car accident during the 1990s. He keeps students awake on Halloween night with the spooky sounds of his skateboard racing up and down the halls. When they stick their heads out of their dorm rooms to ask the noisemaker to take his skateboarding outside, students see a male student riding by on his skateboard; then this ghostly figure mysteriously disappears.

Other ghosts at Chaminade are thought to be the spirits of children, as two of the dorms were used as children's hospitals during World War II. The whispers of young children can be heard at the Hale Hoaloha dorm-where students report hearing little kids' voices in rooms located only on the even side of the third-floor hall. The students report that it sounds like the kids are playing ball, as they hear bouncing sounds and laughter, just as if they were watching kids on a playground.

At the nearby Hale Lokelani dorm, which was also used as a children's hospital during the war, there are frequent reports of deadbolted doors opening and closing. Students say they frequently see ghosts in the rooms and hear strange noises in the middle of the night. Students sleeping in this dorm have awakened because they feel someone putting pressure on their bodies and feel as if they were choking. In Room 319, once a morgue for soldiers during the war, students report seeing ghosts dressed in soldier's attire.

Chaminade University was founded in 1955 by the Society of Mary (Marianists), a Catholic order dedicated to the education of the heart, mind, and soul. Today, Chaminade is a small Catholic university, with a total enrollment of about 1,000 undergraduate and 500 graduate students.

CHAMINADE UNIVERSITY

31449 WAIALAE AVENUE

HONOLULU, HAWAII 96816

Righting Wrongs: The Lady in Gray Continues to Haunt Library over Dispute

Willard Library has been serving the river city of Evansville, Indiana, since it opened its doors in 1885 as the oldest public library building in the state. And some say, probably the most haunted.

Built with a grant by local philanthropist Willard Carpenter, it was formed to be "a public library for the use of the people of all classes, races, and sexes, free of charge forever."

But it's also believed that the ghost of his daughter, Louise Carpenter, dubbed the "Lady in Gray," haunts the library. Her first sighting was in 1937 by a janitor who, while shoveling coal into the basement furnace on a cold snowy night, saw a veiled lady with an unusual glowing gray orb surrounding her. She was gray from head to toe. He fled the building and never returned.

Louise had once sued the library's Board of Trustees, claiming that her father was "of unsound mind and was unduly influenced in establishing Willard Library." She lost the suit and, as a result, her claim to any of the library's property. She felt cheated by the decision. After her death, her spirit returned to the place that caused her so much grief during her life: Willard Library. Those who believe this say that she will continue to haunt the library until the property and its holdings are turned back over to the living heirs of the Willard Carpenter family.

Her anger seems to become particularly active when visitors to the library are just sitting, browsing through the books; suddenly they will feel a cold draft, a creepy cold shiver up their spines, often they smell a strong scent of heavy perfume.

At times, books in the stacks fly off of the shelves by themselves. The library's security motor sensors go off without anyone triggering them. Water faucets are mysteriously turned on. The "Lady in Gray" has been seen fleeing the stacks after a book-throwing episode. She seemingly thinks causing disturbances will get the visitors to vacate the library. The library has even installed cameras called ghost-cams to monitor the areas of the hauntings: one in the research room, the second in the children's room, and the latest installation in the basement.

The library, housed in a beautiful Victorian Gothic building designed by James and Merritt Reid, is near the downtown area of this southwestern Indiana city of 130,000 people, providing a sharp contrast with the modern high-rises and six-lane freeways. Willard Library has been a true icon of the Evansville community for more than 100 years and was inducted into the National Register of Historic Places in 1972.

There are other opinions about whose ghost the famed "Lady in Gray" actually is. Not everyone believes it is Louise

Carpenter. Some believe that the ghost emigrated from a nearby cemetery. Others say that a woman died in the building during its early days and that she liked the library so much that she never left. But, most observers feel that Louise Carpenter, the philanthropist's daughter, is the "Lady in Gray."

WILLARD LIBRARY
21 FIRST AVENUE
EVANSVILLE, INDIANA 47710

UNIVERSITY OF NOTRE DAME
SOUTH BEND, INDIANA

Win One for Gipper the Ghost

They call them the Fighting Irish, and they have a long tradition of excellence as scholars, athletes, and even as celebrities. But at least one famous alumni who has crossed over into the afterlife seems to have a more restless spirit than others and has decided to linger. He is now affectionately known as the ghost of Notre Dame University.

It should be no surprise that the university's world-famous football team would produce its most popular and friendly ghost: legendary football player George Gipp. The star player is said to haunt his old dorm, Washington Hall. Gipp often stayed out after the curfew set by the stern brother who was in charge of the boys in the hall. He was said to have slept on the front steps of the building rather than face the brother's wrath at coming in late. He caught cold, which turned into his fatal case of pneumonia. He died on December 14, 1920, at Saint Joseph Hospital, where upon his deathbed he made his famous remark to Knute Rockne: "Win One for the Gipper."

The mysterious events in Washington Hall began shortly after Gipp's death; students claimed to hear music playing in the building late at night and instruments playing by themselves. Some students claimed to see a very transparent ghostly figure roaming the halls making low moaning sounds. Mysterious footsteps sounded in the halls at all hours, doors slammed when no one was around, and one student claimed that invisible hands pushed him as he was walking down a stairway. Even the skeptical Catholic brothers were convinced that something strange was going on.

Long before the university came into existence, the Pottawattamie Indians inhabited the area and the shorelines of what is now known as the St. Joseph River; they buried their dead in the area of the campus. It is believed that the tribe still inhabits the grounds. Many credible witnesses have reported ghostly images of these Native Americans, especially in the area around Columbus Hall, over the years. Columbus Hall is one of the original, early buildings on the campus. And on numerous occasions the ghostly figures and their spectral horses have been seen riding up and down its stone front steps.

UNIVERSITY OF NOTRE DAME
100 O'SHAUGHNESSY HALL
NOTRE DAME, INDIANA 46556

Triple Suicide at Iowa's Flagship University Leads to Hauntings

For more than 150 years, the University of Iowa has ranked as the state's top institution of higher learning. Established in 1847, the 1,900-acre campus is perhaps best known for its Writers' Workshop, an M.F.A. program founded in 1936 that was the first of its kind in the country and is still the most prestigious. Located in the middle of cornfields, the gray-stone and red-brick buildings rise on bluffs above the winding Iowa River. The university is home to 29,000 Hawkeyes (9,000 graduate and 20,000 undergraduate students).

But it was a triple suicide that caused a paranormal stir at this Midwestern university. The story is that three coeds had fallen in love with the same man and committed a triple suicide on the fourth floor of Currier Hall when they discovered the situation.

The ghosts appear during times when roommates are bickering among themselves. Legend has it the ghosts are tenderhearted and appear to promote friendship and harmony. Those who have felt their spirit say they get the feeling and almost hear someone telling them to talk to each other.

In the married student housing, it is another matter altogether: the ghosts there are not supporting harmony. There have been reports of dishes flying out of the sink and shattering against the walls, tappings from inside the walls, and students having terrible nightmares.

In a variation of the Currier Hall story, a stern-faced older man, "George the Ghost," haunts the Hall Mall. He is said to be the father of a former Currier Hall tenant. And, he's not the most friendly of ghosts: his menacing footsteps and eerie presence send fear down the spines of residents in the Hall Mall year round. Employees say they have never seen George, just heard him. They hear the footsteps coming up the long hallway right to the entrance of the doorway, but no one is ever there.

The campus isn't Iowa City's only haunted spot. Close to campus, Iowa City's Oakland Cemetery is a magnet for students, especially around Halloween, who are searching for spirits and specifically the cemetery's Black Angel statue. According to legend, the nine-foot-tall bronze statue of an angel with outstretched arms turned black shortly after it was erected. It is said that her cold stare will make someone in the group uncomfortable enough to want to leave.

UNIVERSITY OF IOWA

107 CALVIN HALL

IOWA CITY, IOWA 52242

Dorm Demons Continue to Haunt

Fargo is said to be the most haunted city in North Dakota. And it seems that helping to boost that ethereal ranking are the town's halls of academia. Ranking highest on this list is North Dakota State University, where an unsolved murder and a suicide keep ghostly spirits spooking the dormitory halls.

Many college campuses are known for having ghostly and poltergeists activities. That's because students tend to be more open-minded when it comes to hauntings. It is not uncommon for students to have seances and uncover the spirits who crave to be acknowledged. The most common occurrences are lights, faucets, radios, TVs, and computers being tuned on and off, toilets flushing, and objects being moved or seen floating in the air.

In the case of fraternity and sorority houses on campus, many of them were once private homes and mansions with their own history of accidental deaths, murder, and suicide. There are hundreds of stories of ghostly spirits haunting these homes, perhaps reliving a painful past or trying desperately to find their way out.

At Ceres Hall, the apparitions make themselves known on the third floor, where it is said a man hanged himself from a heat pipe during one of the World Wars. It is not unusual to see his ghost disappear through the walls and to reappear in locked rooms. The building's basement also sends unsuspecting visitors racing up the stairs with a strong instinctual feeling of impending danger. The feeling down there, some say, is more evil than ghostly.

In nearby Minard Hall, students say they experience the strange feeling of never being alone and often feel as if someone is staring at them from behind. The temperature in the rooms will suddenly drop and an icy breeze stirs the air.

Fargo also has known poltergeist activity at the Yunker Farm Children's Museum. Deadbolt doors unlock by themselves-one door in particular is repeatedly found unlocked and open, although there is only one key. The elevator in the building often operates by itself. Most visitors feel a sense of a friendly presence; children visiting the museum say they feel as if someone is watching them, but in a nice way.

NORTH DAKOTA STATE UNIVERSITY

1301 12TH AVENUE NORTH

FARGO, NORTH DAKOTA 58105

Guess Who's Coming to Dinner: Culinary Capers Make Good Reading

It certainly makes for interesting history and storytelling. Before being converted, the Hinckley Library in Hinckley, Ohio was the home to Vernon Stouffer, the founder of the Stouffer Foods empire. Though patrons don't exactly report smelling lasagna wafting through the book aisles, the ghosts that haunt the stacks certainly provide food for thought.

After its conversion into a library in 1974, employees reported seeing a young woman in a nineteenth-century-style blue dress after the library is locked up for the night. She would be seen looking out from one of the library's windows. At other times, a man wearing a plug hat was seen peering through the bars of the staircase or standing near the top of the stairway. Employees at the library also say they frequently saw the ghosts of children in the aisles and heard unexplained noises on the upper floor of the former mansion.

Some believe it is not the Stouffer family who haunts but that the library is haunted by earlier residents of the site. The home was built in 1847, and Dr. Orlando Wilcox and his family lived in the house during the Civil War era. According to Judge Webber's *History of Hinckley*, Wilcox was regarded as a walking encyclopedia. He left the practice of medicine and became a noted teacher in the Hinckley area. He wore a plug hat at all times, and is believed to be the ghostly appearance seen by the stairway.

But, Dr. Wilcox is not the only ghostly presence. His daughter, Rebecca, who came upon an untimely death when she was just 30 years old, is said to be the handsome woman seen at the window.

The Hinckley Library location at the Stouffer house was closed in late 2003 due to the deteriorating condition of the floors. There is a new library at 1315 Ridge Road. Even though it's now closed, people say they sometimes see what appears to ghostly spirits walking, or floating, with a light in their hands–one going around the front of the building off Route 303 and the other toward the back off Ridge Road. The Stouffer Library may be closed but the ghosts still reside there.

THE OLD HINCKLEY LIBRARY
ROUTES 3 AND 303
HINCKLEY, OHIO 44233
(NOW CLOSED)

Two Ladies and a Gentleman

Southern Vermont College has a very interesting legacy. Originally, it was a summer home to Edward Everett, the man who created the original Coca-Cola bottle. Later it became a seminary. Today it is a small private liberal arts college.

According to students and faculty there, Everett and his first and second wives haunt the college. Everett's first wife drowned in what is called the upper pond at the top of a hill on campus. She is known as "the Lady in White," because people have reported seeing her in a flowing white gown as she climbs up the hill to the upper pond. She is mainly seen in the early fall, her white gown a contrast to the bright colorful trees in the background. She floats above the ground and as she gets closer to the pond she gradually becomes more transparent and fades away.

The old carriage house, which is today one of the computer labs, is a popular place for an Everett sighting, where he is sometimes joined by his second wife. Doors lock and computers shut off, and the room is reported to be filled with energy and frequent cold spots. It is not uncommon for students to hear wall rapping from the neighboring rooms. Everett himself is rarely seen but he likes to cast shadows while students are at the computer, blocking them from viewing the screen. The carriage house was once was the sleeping quarters for the house staff. It is reported that a maid hanged herself there, which may also add to the ghostly energy.

And Southern Vermont College isn't the only haunted campus around town. At nearby Bennington College, a ghost is said to haunt Jennings Hall, the facility for music students. Students have reported hearing footsteps and voices late at night. It is said that Jennings Hall was the inspiration for the Shirley Jackson novel *The Haunting of Hill House*.

SOUTHERN VERMONT COLLEGE

982 MANSION DRIVE

BENNINGTON, VERMONT 05201

True Confessions: Cast in Stone, Mason Ghost Won't Let His Spirit Stay Walled In

According to tradition, the inspiration for the design of St. Mark's Episcopal Church in Cheyenne, Wyoming, came from the Stoke Poges Church near London. In 1886, the main part of this church was built. But, church members decided they wanted to expand the church in 1925 by adding a grand bell tower.

One day in 1966, a very old man confessed to the church's rector that when he was a young man, he and a fellow Swedish immigrant mason were hired to work on the bell tower of St. Mark's Church. When his fellow mason slipped and fell to his death, he panicked and stuffed the body into an unfinished section of the wall, fitting it into the curvature of the wall. He put a thick layer of cement over the body, sealing it in the wall, then covered the spot with stones.

Starting when the tower had been completed in 1927, from time to time, the eleven twenty-ton carillon bells would mysteriously ring. But there would be no one present in the tower. Now it was clear that there had been a ghost in the church's bell tower.

In addition to the bells ringing, there were reports of muffled indistinguishable talking coming from the walls. Now parishioners found out more about the "voice in the wall" they had been drawn to for years.

In 1979, the bell tower was opened for public tours, which was a very popular event around Halloween. A few years later, a psychic, Ms. Wright, and a deejay from a Cheyenne radio station decided to spend Halloween night broadcasting from the tower. As they climbed the stairway, she was overcome by dreadful feelings; they sensed the presence of a frightening, upset apparition.

While they were in the tower, the bells began to ring by themselves. They also heard a man's voice shouting, "Get out while you still have your mind." Frightened, they left the tower within fifteen minutes. A few minutes later, the bells again rang all by themselves. After a thorough search by police, no human was found. There was no logical explanation for the impromptu bell ringing. These days, the bell tower is closed.

ST MARK'S EPISCOPAL CHURCH
1908 CENTRAL AVENUE
CHEYENNE, WYOMING 82001

PART III

Time-Honored Ghosts

From Battlefields and Cemeteries to Lighthouses and National Parks, Phantoms Make for Ghostly Attractions

Whether it's the battlefields of Gettysburg, an abandoned Arizona penitentiary, or long-deserted lighthouses, ghosts have made their spectral presence known in many places throughout American history. Here, you'll meet dozens of phantoms who've rocked many a jailhouse, led soldiers into battle, manned lighthouses, and who continue to make their afterlife presence known today.

In this chapter, there are selections that are a mix of folklore, real-life investigations, and firsthand accounts of some of the better-known ghost stories in the United States.

We showcase tales of courage that are born on the battlefields-some are famous phantoms, others are unidentified heroes whose bloody conflicts gave rise to their ghosts who continue to haunt the fields of battle. You'll learn about the town of Harpers Ferry, home to the ghost of John Brown, who is known to haunt modern-day tourists. Here, too, is the story of a visitor to Fort Delaware who in 1985 snapped a picture of a Confederate officer standing in an archway. And you'll learn about the famous siege at the Alamo in San Antonio, where few received proper burial, and where a sense of great sadness and despair permeates the mission to this day.

Prisons are another venue where brutality, pain, and misery come to life daily. It's no wonder then that prisons, such as

Yuma Territorial Prison in Arizona, house some not-so-friendly ghosts who torment visitors daily.

Lighthouses-often isolated and lonely places-are also a must-stop refuge for phantoms. You'll read tales of lighthouse keepers and their family members, who, having met an untimely demise, continue to engage in phantom activity.

And most ghost-fearing folks know that cemeteries are definitely off-limits at night unless one is determined to experience the paranormal. Cemeteries have a reputation for hauntings, and we visit some of the ghostliest graveyards in America.

Brimming with poignant and chilling tales about shipwrecks, naval adventure, and just plain good ghost stories, this chapter brings to life a spooky side of American history.

Cemeteries

BACHELOR'S GROVE CEMETERY
MIDLOTHIAN, ILLINOIS

A Grave Situation: Cemetery Has Most Hauntings in Chicago Area

To passersby, it appears to be just a small, abandoned, vandalized, unkempt cemetery in one of Chicago's southern suburbs. But to those in the ghostly know, Bachelor's Grove Cemetery in Midlothian, Illinois, is one of the most haunted cemeteries in America.

Located on a one-acre plot near the Rubio Woods Forest Preserve, Bachelor's Grove is certainly one of Chicago's most active graveyards. Rumor has it that the now-abandoned burial site got its name from the large number of unmarried men who once lived in this western suburb. Though no one has been buried here since the 1960s, it has become a popular site for satanic rituals and voodoo practices. There's also been a great deal of vandalism, including gravestones being defaced or smashed and coffins being dug out and opened.

Always a spooky place, since it opened in the nineteenth century there have been hundreds of ghost sightings. Its history speaks volumes as to why: among other things, Bachelor's Grove Cemetery was a favorite dumping ground of murder victims from gangsters during the 1920s.

The haunted history of the place goes back to its earliest beginnings when the area was set aside as a burial ground, first called Everdon's. In the middle of the nineteenth century, the area became known as "Bachelor's Grove" because there was a settlement of immigrant workers, mostly German, living near the cemetery who had helped build the Illinois-Michigan Canal. The settlers lived on small farms and many of the unmarried men worked at and took care of the farms.

The haunted sightings include a hooded monk; a so-called White Lady of Bachelor's Grove; a farmer and his horse and plow; various cars and other vehicles; men walking out of the lagoon (which was a common dumping place for bodies during the gang wars of the Prohibition era); a ghostly farmhouse; and even a two-headed ghost.

The White Lady appears as a woman dressed entirely in white who is known to walk the grounds of the cemetery during a full moon. The deceased woman rumored to be the White Lady is buried in the cemetery beside her young son. Sometimes the ghostly woman is seen holding a baby in her arms; at other times, she appears to be looking for him.

Another famous Bachelor's Grove ghost is the woman sitting on a gravestone. What makes this ghost so famous is that she was caught on camera and featured in the *Chicago Sun-Times* newspaper in 1991. A very real picture shows the transparent image of a woman sitting comfortably and staring away from the camera out into the woods; it was a black-and-white infrared shot taken of an area where ghost researchers had noticed something unusual.

Just past the fence surrounding the cemetery is a small lagoon that borders the nearby expressway. The story is that this is the spot where gangsters dumped their murder victims during the years of Prohibition. A number of bodies were said to have been found floating in the lagoon here in the Chicago gangster days, so it isn't surprising that the pond is reported to be haunted. There have been sightings of men, dressed in their 1930s gangster-style finery, walking, almost floating, through the lagoon.

Strangely, one ghost linked to the lagoon is said to be a two-headed creature that has been reported on several occasions. No substantive information can be found on this strange apparition. The sinister background of the famous lagoon may be responsible for this ghost sightings, but the reason for his two heads is open to interpretation.

Another well-known ghost of the lagoon is an old farmer who is said to have been pulled into the water by his plow horse in the 1870s. The horse was drowned by the weight of the plow, taking the farmer with it. Two forest rangers spotted the phantom farmer guiding the horse and plow through the wet fields more than one hundred years later.

The ghostly lights of the cemetery and the trail leading through the woods are also well known to researchers. The strange lights on the trail are said to be red in color and move so fast that they leave a streak behind them in the air. The blue orbs of light in the cemetery itself seem to have a form of intelligence, dancing just out of reach of those who pursue them.

Not all ghosts are confined to the area next to the cemetery, and not all of the ghosts are former living beings. On the path leading to the cemetery, a picturesque white farmhouse, usually described as a Victorian farmhouse with a white picket fence and a porch swing, appears and then quickly disappears. Most reports of this phenomenon happened around the 1950s. It's been dubbed "the Phantom Farmhouse."

Even the roads leading to Bachelor's Grove are said to be haunted. For a number of years, witnesses have reported phantom cars that disappear along these roads. Drivers passing by on the nearby expressway outside of the gravel path will come up to a sharp curve in the road. When coming around the curve, they sometimes collide with what seems to be a vintage 1930s gangster car. What they learn after the first shock has passed is that there is no damage, no pain, and no other car.

Abandoned since 1965, there was one burial there in 1989, when the ashes of a local resident were interred on the grounds.

BACHELOR'S GROVE
143RD STREET
MIDLOTHIAN, ILLINOIS 60445
(NOW CLOSED)

Flapper Dances the Nights Away in Ghostly Graveyard

For those who fear ghosts, cemeteries should definitely be off-limits, especially at night.

Reports of hauntings in graveyards have been common since the time of the ancient Greeks.

In Chicago, for example, there are several known haunted graveyards. And one of the most active is Forest Home Cemetery in Forest Park, Illinois.

One of the ghosts is an attractive young woman dressed in the fashion of the Roaring '20s, appropriately dubbed the "Flapper Ghost." She is said to hitch rides on Des Plaines Avenue in Forest Park and then disappear into the cemetery.

According to the story, beginning in the 1920s, the Flapper Ghost would appear at the Melody Mill Ballroom, looking quite alive and human and dancing with the young men. She would ask for a ride home, ask to be dropped off at Forest, saying she lived in the caretaker's house. The flapper would then dash into the cemetery and vanish among the tombstones. In one of the last reported sightings of the flapper ghost, the police investigators walked from the Ballroom toward the cemetery and spotted her. But as they got closer, she again disappeared.

Forest Home Cemetery includes what was once two cemeteries: The Forest Home Cemetery and The Waldheim Cemetery, which adjoined it on the south side. The two merged in 1969, under the name Forest (Waldheim means forest in German). The cemetery is located west of Chicago, and is bordered on the north by the Eisenhower Expressway

Before it was the Forest Cemetery, the land had been a burial ground for the Pottawattamie Indians. Later, a family of white settlers used the small hill containing the burial grounds for the same purpose.

In 1873 German Masonic lodges organized Waldheim Cemetery; Forest Home was established in 1876. Unlike many cemeteries, Waldheim and Forest Home were open to all, not discriminating on the basis of ethnicity or religion, and became very popular with immigrants. Funeral parties and families visiting graves could ride the Chicago and North Western Railroad from the city, transferring to a Des Plaines Avenue streetcar.

FOREST HOME CEMETERY
863 S. DES PLAINES AVENUE
FOREST PARK, ILLINOIS 60130

RESURRECTION CEMETERY
JUSTICE, ILLINOIS

Proud Resurrection Mary
Keeps on Haunting

Talk ghosts in Chicago, and the first thing to pop out of someone's mouth is "Resurrection Mary!"

"Isn't she that cemetery ghost?" your conversation partner will ask. "Yeah, she's famous," the person will enthuse.

Indeed, the legend of Resurrection Mary is one Chicago story that keeps on rolling, anywhere and anytime the conversation turns to things supernatural. Ask almost any Chicagoan and they can tell her story. Even ghost hunters treasure Resurrection Mary as one of their favorites, because they say the story has all the elements of the fantastic-from the beautiful female spirit to actual eyewitness sightings that have yet to be debunked.

There are many vanishing hitchhiker ghost stories in Chicago-some even dating back to horse and buggy days. Mary's story begins in the 1930s when drivers along Archer Avenue started reporting strange encounters with a young woman in a white dress.

The real woman behind the Resurrection Mary moniker is

named Mary Bregavy. She was a young Polish girl who was killed in a car accident in 1939 while going home from a dance at the O'Henry Ballroom, now the Willowbrook Ballroom, down the street from Resurrection Cemetery. Her blonde-haired, blue-eyed ghost makes appearances all along the route to and from the cemetery, and at Resurrection Cemetery and the Willowbrook Ballroom. She has been known to dance with men at the ballroom and ask them for a ride home only to disappear from their cars as they pass the cemetery.

Since her death, folks have spotted Mary hitchhiking on nearby roads and cab drivers have sworn they've picked her up, and just when they are passing Resurrection Cemetery, she disappears.

Many call her Chicago's most famous ghost. The very first account came from a Southside man who died in 1979. When he was a young man, he met a young woman at a local dance club and danced with her the entire evening. Later, she asked for a ride home. As they began to approach the main gates of Resurrection Cemetery, she began to act very strangely. She told him to pull the car off the road. Before he knew what was happening, she darted from the car, ran towards the main gates but disappeared before reaching those gates. He put all of this together and surmised that he had been with a ghost that evening. On a later visit to the home of Mary, the girl he met at the dance, a woman greeted him and told him that her daughter had been dead for some time. He even saw a picture of her sitting on a table and was convinced that she was the same girl he had been with.

Mary has also been hit by a few cars, only to have vanished when the drivers get out to find her. Most of the Mary sightings have come in cold winter months, and many of the motorists have been so shaken that they have appeared at the Justice police station to recount their harrowing experience.

RESURRECTION CEMETERY

7600 ARCHER ROAD

JUSTICE, ILLINOIS 60458

STEPP CEMETERY
BLOOMINGTON, INDIANA

Series of Tragic Events Leads to Lady in Black Spectral Hauntings

Stepp Cemetery is located off Old State Highway 37 in the Morgan-Monroe State Forest outside Bloomington, Indiana. The cemetery is small and lies deep in the forest where light barely ever shines through the thick trees. And it is haunted.

The story of Stepp Cemetery begins in the late 1800s, when settler Rueben Stepp purchased land and proceeded to build a life for his family of nine. The land and weather were rough and many in the small community, including children, perished from influenza, whooping cough, and dysentery. Some believe that the ghostly apparition, always seen in black, is the mother of one of the children whose life was cut short by disease.

The Lady in Black is seen sitting on an old tangled tree stump near a grave, often heard weeping. Park Rangers are often notified of a woman in stress at the cemetery, but when they check no one is there. The description of the ghost by those who have seen her is eerily similar; a woman dressed all in black, with shocking white hair, old but not unattractive.

The most common theory for the Lady in Black is that in the 1930s, during the Great Depression, a man named Jacob moved his family to Bloomington, Indiana, and he found employment at the local rock quarry.

It was hard and dangerous work, but it was work, and employment was scarce at the time. Jacob's wife, Anna, and their daughter, Emily, were happy in their new home and all was well. Until the day that Jacob was killed at the quarry when a dynamite blast went off unexpectedly. Two days later Jacob was buried at Stepp Cemetery.

After Jacob's death, Anna devoted all of her time to her daughter. She became obsessed with her daughter's safety. Anna was very protective of Emily, but she could not keep her at home forever. Just before Emily's seventeenth birthday, she was invited to a dance. Anna reluctantly agreed to let her go. Racing home to meet her curfew, Emily and her date skidded in their car on the rain-soaked highway and were killed in a car crash. Two days later, Emily was buried along-side her father at Stepp Cemetery.

The story is that Anna would go to the gravesides every day, sitting next to the graves and carrying on conversations as if her husband and daughter were still alive. When Anna died a couple of years later, she too was buried at Stepp Cemetery.

Soon afterward, sightings occurred of an older woman

wandering through the cemetery, sitting next to Jacob and Emily's graves. She is dressed in black and is sitting on an old twisted tree stump, as if protecting the graves. Many who have witnessed the spectral sightings of the woman in black remark on the strangeness of the tree stump–it looks like a ghostly chair. If you sit on it, a feeling of coldness comes over you, and legend has it anyone sitting too long on the stump will die within the year.

The Stepp Cemetery is used today only by members of families already buried there. But, many a ghost hunter comes seeking the Lady in Black.

STEPP CEMETERY

OLD HIGHWAY 37

BLOOMINGTON, INDIANA

ST. LOUIS CEMETERY
NEW ORLEANS, LOUISIANA

It's a Voodoo Queen and a Priest Who Haunt a French Quarter Cemetery

A far cry from Mardi Gras, New Orleans, Louisiana, is also known for its hauntings. In fact, it's been called the most haunted city in the United States.

The Old St. Louis Cemetery in the French Quarter hosts

one of the most famous, or infamous, New Orleans ghosts: Marie Laveau, the nineteenth-century Voodoo Queen. Marie was a free woman, not a slave, who had a white father. She became a "Voodoo Legend" in her own lifetime. Many people, both black and white, came to her small house on St. Ann Street for her powerful cure bags of roots, herbs, and charms. She was known for both good and Black (bad) Magic.

Because of the high water table, the tradition in New Orleans was to bury people in tombs and mausoleums, above ground. When Marie died, she was supposedly entombed in the Old St. Louis Cemetery, the most famous of New Orleans' cemeteries, also known as St. Louis Cemetery No. I. There are other theories of where she might be buried, but most Voodoo devotees and curious onlookers believe the unmarked white two-tiered stone tomb is that of her and one of her daughters, Marie II. Tokens of affection and offerings such as coins, pieces of bones, herbs, and flower are routinely left at the gravesite. These are left out of great respect for the Voodoo Queen and the belief that even in death, she will bestow good luck and blessings on the living. Some visitors mark three Xs on her tomb with a piece of chalk, and then ask Marie for a favor.

Many believe Marie returns once a year on St. John's Eve to join with her followers in worship. She has been seen in the graveyard as well as just outside the cemetery. She is recognized by her "Tignon," a knotted handkerchief that she always wore

In the 1930s a reported incident happened in a drugstore near the cemetery. A customer not knowing anything about the famous Voodoo Queen, was talking to the druggist when an old woman came into the drugstore with a "Tignon" and flowing white dress. The druggist took one look at her and ran into the back of the store. The customer turned to the woman and began laughing. She then spoke, asking if he knew who she was. When he replied "No," she slapped him across the face, ran out of the store, and vanished over the cemetery wall.

Others believe Marie Laveau haunts the cemetery in unrecognizable forms. They say she is a large black dog–one that is frequently spotted roaming the grounds–or that she flies over tombs in the guise of a giant black crow.

Certainly Marie's presence in St. Louis Cemetery is one of the best-known tales of New Orleans, but the cemetery does have other spirits.

One such spirit is Father Pere Dagobert. In 1764, New Orleans was ceded to Spain. The French who lived in New Orleans objected, and a rebellion against Spanish rule broke out, led by six French men. The five principal leaders of the rebellion were caught and killed by a Spanish firing squad. The sixth member later died of bayonet wounds. After the six men were dead, Don Alejandro O'Reilly, an Irishman fighting for Spain and commander of the Spanish fleet, ordered that the men not be buried. He ordered that the corpses be left out in the open to rot.

Legend has it that late one night, Father Pere Dagobert, beloved priest of the New Orleans colony was able to arrange a proper burial at the cemetery for the men. These days, visitors say they hear the priest's voice clearly singing in the early morning and that the priest is there to continue to watch over the men.

The Old St. Louis Cemetery is located on the edge of the

French Quarter. For many reasons it is advisable to go there during the day, and with another person or two.

OLD ST. LOUIS CEMETERY

RAMPART STREET

NEW ORLEANS, LOUISIANA 70112

St. James Episcopal Church and Burial Ground
Wilmington, North Carolina

Burial Ground for the Famous, Hauntings Offer Rich History Lesson

As part of the oldest church in Wilmington, North Carolina-St. James Episcopal Church-St. James Cemetery is steeped in rich history. Located at the corner of Fourth and Market Streets, it was an active burial ground from 1745 to 1855.

It is home-or graveyard-to some significant American history makers, among them patriot Cornelius Harnett, remembered for antagonizing the British by reading the Declaration of Independence aloud at the Halifax Courthouse in 1776. He died in a British prison during the war.

America's first playwright, Thomas Godfrey, is also memorialized here.

The cemetery once occupied grounds over which Market

St. James Episcopal Church

- Parish established in 1729 at Brunswick Town (across the river).

- Congregation's present church completed in 1770.

- Church seized in 1781 by Tarleton's Dragoons under Cornwallis. Tarleton had the pews removed, and the church became a stable.

- Original church demolished in 1839 and new building constructed.

- Built in an Early Gothic Revival style with pinnacled square towers, battlements, and lancet windows. Designed by architect Thomas U. Walter, best known for his 1865 cast-iron dome on the U.S. Capitol.

- During the Civil War occupying Federal forces used the church as a hospital.

- A letter written by the pastor asking President Lincoln for reparation still exists. The letter was never delivered, having been completed the day news arrived of Lincoln's assassination.

- Within the church hangs a celebrated painting of Christ (Ecce Homo) captured from one of the Spanish pirate ships that attacked Brunswick Town in 1748.

- Church offices are in the McRae House, built in 1900 from a design by Henry Bacon, who also designed the Lincoln Memorial in Washington, D.C.

Street now stretches, which explains why utility workers periodically (and inadvertently) unearth human remains outside the present burial ground.

The ghosts of Revolutionary War soldiers have been seen, and moaning sounds have been heard, as if from injured soldiers, from around the cemetery. Reports of cold spots near the entryway and orbs of lights floating above the grounds have fascinated ghost hunters.

These spirits are what visitors say continue to haunt the grounds today, making this burial ground a favorite spot on local history and mystery tours. It is open to the public for self-guided tours.

ST. JAMES EPISCOPAL CHURCH AND BURIAL GROUND
25 S. THIRD STREET
WILMINGTON, NORTH CAROLINA

LIVERMORE TOWN AND CEMETERY
LIVERMORE, PENNSYLVANIA

Livermore No More Phantom Town and Classic Horror Film Cemetery Site

Livermore, the town, no longer exists. The canal town was established in the early 1800s, situated along the Connemaugh River in Western Pennsylvania for more than a century and a half. However, frequent flooding discouraged many from staying, and in the 1950s, the Army Corps of Engineers purchased all of the property along the river and closed the town to make way for the Connemaugh Dam between New Alexander and Saltsburg, Pennsylvania. Livermore the town became the Connemaugh River Lake, part of the flood-control project for the Dam.

When the town was flooded, the Army Corps of Engineers did not tear down all of the buildings. In fact, when the moon is bright and the water is clear, you can still see the tops of chimneys and a church steeple in the lake. Strange noises are often heard coming from the water.

Before the dam was built, the Army Corps moved the dead bodies and gravestones from the Livermore Cemetery to its present location on higher grounds. It is believed that the ghosts of those whose graves were moved now roam the nearby woods, restlessly looking for their original graves and homes.

There have been many incidents of ghostly spirits, dressed in their nineteenth-century clothing, seen walking in the woods; and there are reports of cold spots, chilling moans, and a sense of being followed as you walk through the area.

Be careful if you go walking there. There are reports of wild dogs, howling and attacking, driven mad by the evil that lurks about.

There are those who tell of seeing a phantom house that appears and disappears. Evil spirits reside in the phantom house-the house and the town were supposedly cursed by a resident witch who was burned to death by the townspeople.

A famous horror film graveyard scene was filmed at the

Livermore Cemetery; in fact, the sign to the cemetery is the same one captured in George A. Romero's *Night of the Living Dead*. Romero, who grew up in Pittsburgh, must have felt the strange energy surrounding the town that no longer exists.

If you do visit the area, make sure you obey all posted signs—due to the notoriety of the area, the police enforce all posted restrictions and trespassing signs.

LIVERMORE TOWN, FOUR MILES WEST OF BLAIRSVILLE,
PENNSYLVANIA
INTERSECTION OF ROUTES 22 & 982
LIVERMORE CEMETERY, THREE MILES NORTH OF INTER-
SECTION ON LIVERMORE ROAD
(NO TRESPASSING ALLOWED)

Lighthouses

Shining a Light on the Ghostly Guardian of the Lighthouse

Perched on a finger of land more than 400 feet above the sea, with the Pacific Ocean on one side and San Diego Bay on the other, the Old Point Loma Lighthouse was built in 1854. It was abandoned before the end of the century, when the New Point Loma Lighthouse was completed. Today, it is a popular tourist attraction.

When visitors enter on the first floor, everything seems calm. But looks can be deceiving. It is soon apparent that although former lighthouse keeper Robert Israel, who lived there more than 100 years ago, is not seen–he is heard.

Israel leaves his imprint in the heavy footsteps heard both

in the kitchen and living room. Visitors feel cold spots when they are ascending or descending the steps to the tower. Many report the sensation of being pushed back as they try to mount the steps in the narrow hallway leading up to the tower.

Even spookier are the sounds of a low moan that are heard in the bedroom, where the long-departed lighthouse keeper's uniform is still laid out on the bed. It's believed that he is angry because he no longer has his job, and he wants to wear the uniform.

Point Loma is in itself unique, tucked away from the main portion of the City of San Diego. Here, atop the hill, visitors can see the entire San Diego Bay. When the famed America's Cup was hosted here, visitors came to this perch for the best viewing of the race.

The Old Point Loma Lighthouse was built here as one of the original eight West Coast lighthouses built in the nineteenth century. Its 40-foot tower rises from the center of the keeper's house. Today, the Old Point Loma Lighthouse is the centerpiece of the Cabrillo National Monument and is open to the public for tours.

THE OLD POINT LOMA LIGHTHOUSE
CABRILLO NATIONAL MONUMENT
POINT LOMA
SAN DIEGO, CALIFORNIA

History of the Old Point Loma Lighthouse

NOVEMBER 15, 1855: The light in the tower of the Old Point Loma Lighthouse shined for the first time, marking the beginning of more than three decades in which the Lighthouse has helped to ensure safe maritime activities in San Diego Bay.

1871: Robert Israel was appointed Assistant Lighthouse Keeper; three years later, he was promoted to Keeper.

1891: The fog-shrouded light finally bowed to the new lighthouse located 100 yards away on the shore. The early west coast lighthouses were built high up on hills, as was the custom in New England, but this tactic didn't work in California, as its beacon was not visible through the low-lying Pacific coast fog. After closing, the unused building was abandoned and fell into disrepair.

1913 TO 1933: The Old Point Loma Lighthouse underwent several minor restorations, but because authorities were considering tearing it down, it was still in disrepair.

OCTOBER 14, 1933: Cabrillo National Monument, which included the old lighthouse, was transferred to the National Park Service. Restoration was begun.

WORLD WAR II: The U.S. Navy used the Old Point Loma Lighthouse as a signal tower to direct ships into San Diego Harbor.

AFTER WORLD WAR II: The lighthouse was opened as a museum staged to depict the period of the 1800s when Mr. and Mrs. Robert Israel, the last lighthouse keepers, lived and worked in the building.

2001: The National Park Service begins a plan to restore the area around the lighthouse to its original late nineteenth-century appearance.

Phantom of the Lighthouse Creates Ghostly Pursuits

Probably the best-known part of this station's history and lore is the lighthouse's infamous ghost, Ernie. It's been claimed that in the 1920s or 1930s, a lighthouse keeper learned that his wife had run off with the captain of the Block Island ferry. Distraught, the keeper-known only as Ernie-committed suicide by jumping to the rocks below.

There's no record of either event, but that doesn't stop the folklore. Ernie's ghostly presence is often felt through unexplainable activity at the lighthouse. Doors have been known to open and close mysteriously, decks have swabbed themselves, televisions have turned themselves off, and, at times, the foghorn turns on and off for no reason. Securely tied boats have mysteriously been set adrift. All of this is attributed to Ernie. It's believed that his spirit just can't rest and that he haunts the house continuing to search for his wife.

In 1987, New London Ledge Lighthouse became the last lighthouse on Long Island Sound to be automated. On the last day before automation, a Coast Guardsman entered in the log:

This one-of-a-kind building was one of the last lighthouses built in New England, and it represents a rare case of an early 20th century offshore lighthouse that is not of cast-iron construction. The stately red brick building with its mansard roof and granite detailing makes a striking picture standing off by itself near the entrance to Connecticut's New London Harbor, at the extreme eastern end of Long Island Sound.

The lighthouse owes its unique architecture and distinctive French Second Empire style to the wealthy homeowners who lived on the shoreline. They wanted the structure to reflect the ambiance of their own homes.

The lighthouse was at first called Southwest Ledge Light, but the name was changed to avoid confusion with the lighthouse of the same name in New Haven Harbor.

When it was first lighted, *The New London Day* reported that the light could be seen up to 18 miles away. The characteristic signal was three white flashes followed by a red flash every 30 seconds. A fog signal was added in 1911, replacing the one at New London Harbor Light. Coast Guard crews lived at the lighthouse from 1939 until its automation in 1987.

NEW LONDON LEDGE LIGHTHOUSE FOUNDATION

P.O. BOX 855

NEW LONDON, CONNECTICUT 06320

(860) 437-3423

Stairway to Heaven: St. Augustine Lighthouse Ghosts Enchant Visitors

Just a mere 219 steps, and visitors to the St. Augustine Lighthouse in Florida have reached the top. If they're not too pooped they're in for more than just a magnificent view when they reach the top.

This black-and-white striped beauty was completed in 1874 and is one of a half dozen lighthouses still open to the public throughout Florida. (At one point there were thirty lighthouses beaming their light into the darkness).

Like most lighthouses, it eventually deteriorated from the wear and tear of the seawater and winds. But in the 1980s the lighthouse was restored. And that's when the fun began. Three ghosts–a small girl, a presence in the basement, and an unidentified man–suddenly made their presence known.

Not much is known about who these ghosts are or where they came from, but the small girl is thought to be a child who was hit and killed by a nearby train around 1900. There is a ghostly presence felt in the basement of the light keeper's house, and there have been sightings of an unidentified man, who is said to have hanged himself at the lighthouse in early years and continues to haunt the premises.

During the construction work, when the lighthouse and the adjacent keeper's house were being restored, workers spent the nights there to protect it from vandals. Reports say they would wake up in the middle of the night to see a small girl in old-fashioned clothes watching them. She would then vanish. They would also sense someone watching them during the workday and would look up and see the apparition of the man hanging from the rafters. The spirit in the basement was never seen, but workers all reported an uneasy feeling when they were in the basement alone, especially at night. There have also been stories of footsteps on the lighthouse stairs when no one was in the building. Once, when the lighthouse museum was being rearranged, a maintenance man lifted one end of a bench to move it out of the way. Before he could walk around to lift the other side, it rose up in the air and moved itself. Today, the lighthouse and light keeper's house are open to the public for tours. Visitors to the lighthouse will hear these tales discussed openly by the museum guides.

St. Augustine Florida is one of America's oldest and most haunted cities. Its unique and often turbulent history has spawned more than four hundred years' worth of shadowy figures. According to local legend, there are numerous ghosts and strange goings-on throughout the town, not just at its lighthouse.

Some say there are so many spirits because the town itself holds so much rich history. The Spanish founded the town of St. Augustine in 1565, some 42 years before the English col

LIGHTHOUSE LORE

The black-and-white color scheme, with a red top, is St. Augustine's distinguishing navigational day mark. All lighthouses also have a night mark, called a signature. The St. Augustine night mark is a short white flash, every thirty seconds. By viewing the signature, mariners can determine their position in the darkness.

onized Jamestown and 55 years before the Pilgrims set foot on Plymouth Rock. It has been continuously occupied since that time.

ST. AUGUSTINE LIGHTHOUSE AND MUSEUM
81 LIGHTHOUSE AVENUE
ST. AUGUSTINE, FLORIDA 32080
(904) 829-0745

First Lady Continues to Shine Her Light

Once a pair of twin lighthouses, the lone-lasting Plymouth Lighthouse at Gurnet Point is said to be haunted by the ghost of America's first woman lighthouse keeper.

Hannah Thomas became the first known female lighthouse keeper in the late eighteenth century when her husband, John, the then light keeper, was killed in the Revolutionary War.

Thomas had built the lighthouse and its twin on their property in 1769. Its twin is no longer there and the existing lighthouse has been rebuilt three times: in 1803, 1843, and 1924. The latest incarnation of the tower is still standing, but it is automated and no longer needs residents to keep it running.

But Hannah and her friendly haunting still keep watch over the lighthouse and its visitors.

When a team of professional lighthouse photographers spent the night at the house adjacent to the tower, they were awoken by the apparition of the upper portion of a woman's body floating above the bed. The ghost was wearing old-fashioned clothing that fit close around her neck, and had long dark hair that fell to her shoulders. No mistake, historians say. The ghost is Hannah, continuing to rule the roost.

The Gurnet is located on a spit of land north of Plymouth, Massachusetts. It sticks out into the Atlantic Ocean. Sometimes it is accessible with a four-wheel drive vehicle, but if it's high tide or the weather is bad, it is unreachable.

Many things happened in the area near that lighthouse, before and after it was built. Some say the Vikings landed there more than one thousand years ago. Others say that there is an Indian burial ground near the lighthouse. It is so close to Plymouth, some believe that Pilgrims most likely came there as well as sailors and sea captains.

Hannah, the Plymouth Lighthouse's ghost, and her story have been the subject of a documentary on ghosts and lighthouses for the Learning Channel, a program often shown around Halloween.

PLYMOUTH LIGHTHOUSE
PLYMOUTH, MASSACHUSETTS 02331

Lighthouse Caretaker Still Here . . . in Spirit

There are several possible explanations for the amber light seen flashing from the tower of an abandoned light-house on Lake Huron near Alpena, Michigan.

But, for many, there is no mystery about the source of light. It's the ghost of George Parris, who lived in the house attached to the lighthouse from 1977 until 1991, when he died of a heart attack. George is a modern ghost by ghost standards; others say it's not George who causes the light and the screaming heard on windy nights, but rather the wife of an earlier lighthouse keeper.

The screams, they say, are the cries of the wife of Patrick Garrity, an earlier lighthouse keeper at this historic site. Patrick and his wife did their duty and lived in this isolated lighthouse. It is rumored that the isolation drove Garrity's wife insane and that he kept her locked up so nobody would know about her mental illness. Today, she is said to cry out in pain, especially on stormy evenings, when the bad weather spooks her spirit.

Other locals agree the lighthouse is haunted, not only by Parris and Garrity but by a third ghost-the daughter of one of the other old lighthouse keepers.

Presque Isle is a thin strip of land sticking out from the shore of Lake Huron near Alpena. The peninsula is now well-known as a four-season outdoor vacation spot hunting, fishing, boating, and cross-country skiing in the winter, are popular activities..Old Presque Isle Lighthouse was built near the base of the peninsula in 1840 and gave 30 long years of service before being replaced by the New Presque Isle Lighthouse. It was then abandoned.

George Parris and his wife Lorraine moved into the small house attached to the lighthouse in 1977, where they looked after the grounds and provided tours for vacationers. Lorraine, who continued to live there after George's death, believes George's spirit is still at the lighthouse protecting the property. It was after George's death in 1991 that the mysterious amber lights began appearing.

Some skeptics say the amber light that shines at night are just reflections from passing boats; others say that the light is visible even on cloudy nights and is indeed that of a ghost, or one of the ghosts. What is known is that Parris, a Coast Guard officer and electrician by trade, went into the tower in June 1979 and disconnected all the wiring, leaving the unused tower without a source of electricity to produce the flicker.

One visitor, a little girl, had climbed to the top of the tower and was talking and giggling when she came back down. Asked whom she had been talking to, she replied, "To the man in the tower." Later, when the girl was in the cottage and saw a portrait of white-haired Parris, she told his widow it was the man she had seen in the tower.

Today, Presque Isle Lighthouse is an inactive museum.

PRESQUE ISLE LIGHTHOUSE

LAKE HURON

PRESQUE ISLE, MICHIGAN

HECETA HEAD LIGHTHOUSE
FLORENCE, OREGON

Lights, Cameras . . . Ghost Action

It's been the backdrop for several films and a made-for-TV movie. It's got its own folklore and has become popular storytelling subject for locals. It's rated as the strongest light on the Oregon coast, with 1.2-million candlepower. But, it's a ghost story that seems to have earned it the most notoriety.

Pronounced "He-see-ta," the lighthouse was built in 1894 and named for the explorer Captain Don Bruno de Heceta of the Spanish Royal Navy, who explored the Northwest coast around 1775. It is perched on a magnificent headland in the Suislaw National Forest in Florence, Oregon.

The ghost is believed to be the mother of an infant girl who fell off the cliffs and died during the 1890s. Caretakers, college students, visitors, and construction workers have claimed that strange unexplained occurrences have taken place inside the house-with appearances also by the mother, supposedly in search of her baby. It is unclear exactly how the young baby lost her life falling off the cliff, but her body was discovered on the rocks below and a small stone near the lighthouse is thought to mark the baby's grave.

The mother, said to be returning in search of her baby, appears in the form of a woman shrouded in a cloud of gray smoke. This has earned her the nickname "Gray Lady."

How this grievous mother manifests herself differs from sighting to sighting. Some have heard screams; some have found things in the lighthouse moved or missing. A worker cleaning attic windows noticed a reflection in the glass and turned to face the eternal visage of a silver-haired woman in a long, dark dress. On another occasion, this worker broke one of the attic windows from the outside but refused to go in to clean up the glass. That night the couple living there heard sounds in the attic and the next day discovered the glass neatly swept into a pile.

The Gray Lady's name is reported to be Rue. She is said to turn lights on and off and pace the floorboards, particularly in the attic, where a latched window is often found mysteriously open. She becomes particularly agitated during any renovations-some say she worries that she'll be forced to vacate and leave her child behind.

Today, Heceta Head Lighthouse is a popular draw for vacationers. The lighthouse is located in Devil's Elbow State Park, which is part of the Suislaw National Forest. While the ghost and B&B draw visitors, nearby is another popular tourist site: Sea Lion Caves, located one mile south of the lighthouse, which is the only mainland site for viewing wild sea lions up close.

Placed on the National Register of Historic Places in 1978, the lighthouse was recently restored, and opened for tours; the nearby lighthouse keeper's house is now a bed and breakfast with three guest rooms.

HECETA HEAD LIGHTHOUSE

91560 HIGHWAY 101

FLORENCE, OREGON 97439

B&B: (541) 547-3696

Battlefields and Military Bases

FORT DELAWARE
PEA PATCH ISLAND, DELAWARE

Pentagon Military Fortress, Home to Dungeon and Ghosts

Wartime habitats, especially those that date back as far as the Civil War, are often infested with the spirits of soldiers whose cries of death, devastation, and despair continue to stand guard over these military bases.

That's why visitors can't let the pastoral setting of Fort Delaware in Delaware State Park fool them. Though it's certainly picturesque and a great tourist destination, under its sweeping lawns and parade grounds lies a dungeon that once held Civil War prisoners, spirits intent on making themselves known today. That of course means one thing: it is ripe ground for ghostly goings-on. And, that's exactly what it has become, a home for the dungeon ghosts.

Fort Delaware is one of Delaware's state parks, created in 1951. On the National Register of Historic Places; it was originally built to protect the ports of Wilmington and Philadelphia.

The Union fortress once served as a prison for Confederate prisoners of war. In fact, during the Civil War 2,700 prisoners died there, due to overcrowded conditions and disease. Some died trying desperately to escape, and many were caught and put into solitary confinement in dark and dreary dungeons. Today, moaning sounds and clanging chains are heard here. Under the ramparts and on the parade grounds, cold spots and spectral visions of fleeing Confederate soldiers have been seen and felt by visitors. One such visitor took a photo of a soldier who was dressed in a Confederate officer's uniform, apparently not willing to go to the other side.

Beyond the civil war, it was home for decades to all kinds of prisoners, including not only soldiers, but pirates as well. Now, it seems that the ghosts of pirates who were imprisoned before the Civil War are also hanging around Fort Delaware. A park ranger was taken aback one day to see a pirate, dressed in a beautiful green silk shirt and white silk pants, sitting by a window at the fort, looking out. The restless spirits who haunt Fort Delaware are a sad reminder of the horror of war and the horrible events that shaped and took lives.

Today, Fort Delaware is a popular tourist attraction. From the parking area in Delaware City, visitors take a ferry to Pea Patch Island. A jitney provides transport from the island dock to the granite and brick fortress. Authentically clad guides begin the visitor's journey back to times of yesteryear.

Pea Patch Island also features many natural treasures. The island is a summer home to nine different species of herons, egrets, and ibis. The remote marshes provide an outstanding habitat for one of the largest wading-bird nesting areas on the East Coast.

FORT DELAWARE
PEA PATCH ISLAND
DELAWARE CITY, DELAWARE
(302) 834-7941

ANDERSONVILLE PRISON
AND ANDERSONVILLE NATIONAL CEMETERY
ANDERSONVILLE, GEORGIA

Civil War Prison Continues to Haunt

Andersonville, or Camp Sumter as it was officially known, was one of the largest of the Confederate military prisons established during the Civil War. It was one of the most overcrowded and crude prisons of that time.

Back in early 1864, when the war was going poorly for the South, a portion of this hard-baked landscape was walled off as a stockade, some 1,620 feet long and 779 feet wide. For fourteen months, more than 45,000 Union soldiers were confined behind the walls. Thirteen thousand of the inmates died. It was a filthy, stinking, disease-ridden place where soldiers died from malnutrition, poor sanitation, and exposure.

Many locations are haunted because of the tragedy that took place there-Andersonville is no exception. Ghosts are found in this location simply because of the nature of ghosts themselves. Many violent deaths occurred at Andersonville, and the area will always hold some spirits and psychic energy. Psychic investigators have reported that the meters go off the scale when they attempt to measure the psychic energy levels. Some visitors have been completely spooked when cold spots pass by, causing intense shivers.

At times, ghosts of hundreds of these prisoners are heard crying out in misery; the former prison is said to be one of the more haunted sites in the country. Many believe that the souls of the prisoners are continuing to cry out to give testimony to the horrific conditions and human suffering that was endured there.

For more than one hundred years, park staff, visitors, and even local people driving by the site have reported ghostly figures, unusual sounds, and strange smells. There are also reports of hearing musket fire at night. And, the men called the Andersonville Raiders-six Union soldier prisoners condemned to death and hung, have been seen roaming the grounds in the late hours of the night.

The Andersonville Prison's awful conditions were said to be caused by the South's deteriorating economic conditions, an inadequate transportation system, and the need to dedicate all available resources to the army. The Confederate government was unable to provide adequate housing, food, clothing, and medical care to their Federal captives. These conditions, along with a breakdown of the prisoner exchange system, resulted in much suffering and a high mortality rate.

Andersonville National Cemetery was established on July 26, 1865, right after the prison closed, to provide a permanent place for those who died in military service for our country. The initial interments, beginning in February 1864, were of those who died in the nearby prisoner of war camp. The cemetery, with row after row of white stone markers placed only inches apart, is a visible reminder of what happened just a few hundred yards away and more than a hundred years ago.

Today, Andersonville National Historic Site is the only park in the National Park System to serve as a memorial to American prisoners of war throughout our nation's history. The 515-acre park consists of the historic prison site and the National Cemetery. Dedicated to the men and women of this country who have suffered captivity, the National Prisoner of War Museum opened at Andersonville in 1998.

ANDERSONVILLE NATIONAL HISTORIC SITE
496 CEMETERY ROAD
ANDERSONVILLE, GEORGIA 31711
(229) 924-0343

Phantom Ghosts Still Doing Active Duty at Closed New York Air Force Base

The Plattsburgh Air Force Base has been closed since 1993, but some of the ghosts that haunt the site still think they are providing service to their country.

Since it was closed, there has been activity at the base, an environmental clean-up effort to clean the fuel-soaked soil, and plans to open a new airport utilizing the old hangars and landing strips.

The site has history: at the time of the Battle of Plattsburgh during the War of 1812, an army base was established there. The area around Plattsburgh also saw its share of fighting during the Revolutionary War and the French and Indian War.

Many ghostly encounters happened when the base was still an active Air Force base, and have increased since the official closing. Thus the reports from workers, engineers, and police of the many spirits that decided to stay on and make their presence known. There are many reports of cold spots, orbs and strobe-like lights, apparitions of French and Indian

War soldiers, sudden loud noises, sounds of soldiers marching and horses, alarms going off for no reason, and officers patrolling having a sense of being followed.

The old gym on the base was once a morgue, used during earlier wars for storing dead bodies. When the gym was still in use, it was notorious for the wild pounding on doors coming from the basement where the morgue had been located, and footsteps overhead coming from unoccupied floors. When the base was being used for training Security Police K-9 units, the dogs would act up whenever they were taken too close to the basement of the old gym.

The entrance to the old Air Force base had two pillars, and there have been sightings of Revolutionary War-era soldiers keeping guard there, marching between the pillars. In the base cemetery called Old Side, security police have reported seeing apparitions of soldiers wandering through the graveyard.

Whatever the development plans may be for the old Air Force base, the spirits that have guarded, worked at, and haunted the grounds for hundreds of years are sure to keep up their ghostly habits.

PLATTSBURGH AIR FORCE BASE

PLATTSBURGH, NEW YORK

(NOW CLOSED)

Pennsylvania Battleground's Ghosts Most Active in Country

It's said to be one of the most haunted places in America. And when the numbers are counted-over 50,000 people lost their lives on the battlefield near Gettysburg during the Civil War-it makes sense that the siren of souls that continue to call out in eternity is especially loud.

Since July 1863, this chorus of ghosts has served as a reminder of the bloody Civil War battle that took place near the town of Gettysburg, Pennsylvania. The ghosts are a reminder of those tens of thousands of people who lost their lives at this site-where more deaths occurred than any other site on North American soil. Because Gettysburg is ripe with paranormal activity, numerous tour group companies have sprung up to show tourists the spookiest spots and share the spine-chilling tales and legends.

Today, Gettysburg is full of ghosts and dozens of spots where these ghosts make themselves known. Some of the ghosts appear as soldiers who are still fighting on the battle-field. There is a wooded area where sounds of a marching band, phantom Civil War music, is common. Other visitors report experiencing overwhelming feelings of danger that often overcome them during tours of the battlefield. The ghosts help visitors imagine what it must have been like on this once bloody war zone.

There are several popular ghost tours. One is Baltimore Street, which takes visitors to the National Cemetery, where spirits of the buried soldiers are said to linger. Tales are told of an apparition known to descend the gatehouse's stairs, as well as the cries of babies heard from the site of a long-gone orphanage. It has been said that spirits of Union and Con-federate soldiers sometimes appear to frighten guests at the house that Abraham Lincoln traveled past to deliver the Get-tysburg Address.

On the Carlisle Street tour, guides talk about the "bizarre poltergeist activity" that has occurred there since the Civil War. They take visitors to a building where actors have said they saw ghostly visions of "the General" watching them per-form. Another building features a modern elevator that is said to have taken unsuspecting passengers back in time to a Civil War hospital.

On a third tour, along Seminary Ridge, visitors learn about the house in which a young soldier was buried alive beneath a pile of corpses for many days before he was removed. Many years after the soldier's death, however, his spirit is said to have remained in the house.

Indeed, spirits roam the streets and historic buildings of

downtown Gettysburg. They wander day and night, spooking this popular tourist town year-round.

The battlefield and cemetery-now a national park-are among the most haunted sites. The Wills House and specifically its Lincoln Room Museum is also a popular tourist attraction and popular haunted site in Gettysburg. It is said that Abraham Lincoln was the guest of attorney David Wills at this home the night before giving his immortal Gettysburg Address.

Some of the other haunted places in town include: Cashtown Inn, built in 1797, which served as the first stagecoach stop west of Gettysburg and the Confederate headquarters; General Lee's Headquarters' Museum, where Lee stayed during the war; and the American Civil War Museum, where life-sized dioramas of the Civil War-and their ghostly spirits-bring the museum back to life.

But the area is best known for just three days-July 1, 2, and 3, 1863-the Battle of Gettysburg. The Soldiers' National Cemetery at Gettysburg was dedicated on November 19, 1863, when President Abraham Lincoln delivered his immortal Gettysburg Address.

On February 11, 1895, Gettysburg National Military Park was established as a memorial to the armies that fought this great battle. Gettysburg National Military Park incorporates nearly 6,000 acres, with 26 miles of park roads and more than 1,400 monuments, markers, and memorials. Each year, nearly 2 million people make the pilgrimage to this venerable site, the largest battlefield shrine in America. Visitors come to see for themselves the spot where thousands fought and died for their cause, and the spot where President Lincoln spoke and still speaks to us today.

GETTYSBURG NATIONAL MILITARY PARK

GETTYSBURG, PENNSYLVANIA

(717) 334-1124

GHOSTS OF GETTYSBURG TOUR HEADQUARTERS

271 BALTIMORE ST.

GETTYSBURG, PENNSYLVANIA 17325

(717) 337-0445

THE ALAMO
SAN ANTONIO, TEXAS

Remember the Alamo: How Could You NOT, with All of These Ghosts?

It was during the eighteenth century that Spanish officials built the Alamo as a Catholic mission. The Alamo compound was later used as a military post in the early 1800s when the Spanish stationed a cavalry unit there. The Alamo played important roles in both the ten-year war for Mexican independence from Spain and in the Texas Revolution against Mexico.

It was during the famous siege, which took place during

the Texas War of Independence, that two hundred Alamo defenders, led by Colonel William B. Travis, lost their lives-among them were Davy Crockett and Jim Bowie. At least six hundred Mexican soldiers also lost their lives in the battle. Few bodies received proper burial; many were thrown into the San Antonio River or incinerated in mounds. It's no wonder that the site of the Alamo is one rife with reports of ghosts and mysterious goings-on. The sheer number of dead is thought to evoke the pervasive supernatural occurrences that have been reported there over the last century.

Indeed, today this mission, turned fortress, turned national shrine is infused with the spirits of the men who fought there and continue to haunt. Some visitors say they are overwhelmed by feelings of sadness that continue to pervade the mission today. Many say they leave crying, not fully understanding the reason for their tears. Others say they feel as if they actually know the souls for whom are crying, as if their spirits entered inside them during their visit.

And then there are the ghosts that visitors see.

One of the most-repeated stories is the ghost of a small blond-haired boy that is seen from time to time in the left upstairs window of the Alamo mission house, now the gift shop. According to legend, the little boy may have been evacuated during the siege and perhaps returns again and again to the place where he last saw his relatives. Though he is seen year-round, he is reported appearing most often in late February, the time when the siege began.

Every March, people living near the Alamo say they hear the sounds of horses' hooves on the pavement; it is said that it is the spirit of James Allen, the last courier to leave the Alamo, trying to report back to Colonel Travis.

Today, the Alamo is a national shrine and museum. But few visitors, most of whom grew up with the Hollywood version of the Alamo story, realize it is one of the most haunted locales in America. The Alamo monument and museum are memorials to the defenders of the Alamo.

THE ALAMO

300 ALAMO PLAZA

SAN ANTONIO, TEXAS 78299

(210) 225-1391

Parks, Prisons, and Outdoor Places

Jailhouse Rock: In the Middle of Nowhere, Ghosts Heat Things Up

It's not hard to understand why ghosts are said to haunt former prisons. Prisons hold some of the most hardened and vicious types in humanity and carry a lot of pain and human suffering in their walls. It is no wonder that residents of the spirit world are holed up in prisons. The ghosts of the Yuma Territorial Prison ("the Old Territorial Prison") in Arizona are no exception. And they don't let visitors forget that they are on the grounds of what was once a state penitentiary.

One ghost likes to pinch people who visit "the hole," a cell with no light where prisoners were thrown into solitary confinement. And, some say the ghosts are especially drawn to playing jokes on children who visit. They also like to move the cash around–especially dimes–in the museum's cash drawers. Not so many years ago, a reporter from *Arizona Highways* wanted to do a story about the prison, and wanted to spend two days and nights in the "dark cell." Within a couple of hours, she was calling for help, claiming that another "person" was in the cell with her!

Here, ghosts make sure they remind visitors of the sadness and sorrow of life in a prison. Visitors say even if they didn't see the ghosts, they feel their presence in powerful ways and can almost imagine the misery of life as a prisoner in these cells.

Located on Prison Hill Road in Yuma, it was the choice place for a prison. In the territorial days, Yuma was (and still is) one of the hottest and driest places in the United States. It was situated in the desert, in the middle of nowhere-one of most isolated places in the country.

The Yuma Territorial Prison, also known as "Hell Hole" opened in the Arizona desert on July 1, 1876, when the first seven inmates entered the prison. They were locked into the new cells that they had built themselves.

Prisoners were sent from all over the country to Yuma and placed in small cells. The temperature usually soared to above 100° F in the summer. Prisoners were chained to the stone floors and walls in the dark cells.

The prisoners built a new prison in Florence, Arizona, and the last prisoners were transferred from the Yuma Territorial Prison on September 15, 1909, when it was officially closed. Today, the cells, dark cell, main gate, and guard tower are all that remain of the original prison, and the grounds of Yuma have been transformed into a historical state park.

YUMA TERRITORIAL PRISON STATE HISTORIC PARK

1 PRISON HILL ROAD

YUMA, ARIZONA 85364

(928) 783-4771

Jailhouse Rock: The Ghost of Alcatraz Still Rocks

It is considered the most famous of America's prisons. Its movie credits give testimony to its popularity. The list seems endless: *The Rock, Birdman of Alcatraz, Dead Man Walking, Murder in the First,* to name a few.

Today, Alcatraz is a popular tourist attraction and national park in the San Francisco Bay, with more than 1 million visitors each year. In the nineteenth century, it was an army fort; it began holding prisoners during the Civil War in 1861. Then, during the 1900s, civilian prisoners were sent there; by 1934, it was a federal prison. There, some of society's most hardened prisoners were sent, as it was considered inescapable. The guest roster included Robert "the Birdman" Stroud, George "Machine Gun" Kelly, and Chicago crime boss Al Capone. The prison was the site of many murders, suicides, and beatings, and also a place where many inmates died or were killed trying to escape; Alcatraz was finally closed in 1963.

But its legacy remains strong and its ghosts continue to

haunt the thousands of visitors each day who take a ferry from Fisherman's Wharf across the bay to get a firsthand glimpse of this infamous institution. Guards and tour guides report hearing sounds of cells being opened and closed, footsteps, whistling, screams, and voices echoing down the halls. Visitors have heard moans, agonized cries, and chains rattling in cell blocks A, B, and particularly C. A psychic who visited the site claimed to identify the unruly spirit of a man named "Butcher" inhabiting the place. Prison records confirm that an inmate in the laundry area of cellblock C killed Abie Maldowitz, a mob hit man nicknamed Butcher.

The D cellblock, where prisoners were held in solitary confinement, and where guests can enter the spooky four-by-eight-inch cellblocks, is haunted as well. Most visitors report feeling a really creepy feeling in this wing of the prison, one that sends chills up their spines. Confinement in the D cellblock was particularly harrowing and those who disobeyed would be sent there for seven days.

Many Rangers and Park Service staff have recounted stories of cell doors mysteriously closing and opening, unexplainable sounds and loud noises, a feeling of being watched, and a sense of terrible pain and suffering. Many psychic investigators and ghost hunters have picked up on the enormous amount of energy surrounding the prison and in the walls and rooms, and the sense of the tortured souls driven mad by the hard rock that was Alcatraz.

ALCATRAZ ISLAND
GOLDEN GATE NATIONAL RECREATION AREA
SAN FRANCISCO, CALIFORNIA
(415) 705-5555

Did Captain Kidd Bury His Treasure on Charles Island in 1699?

Charles Island, part of the Silver Sands State Park in Connecticut, has a long and complex history. The sole access to the island is a causeway that only surfaces from the sea at low tide. Today, it is a place where tragedy after tragedy, and a series of mysterious events, underscore beliefs that this island is truly haunted.

Legend has it that Captain Kidd buried part of his treasure here and part on one of several other islands along the Connecticut and Massachusetts coasts, all places that the notorious pirate visited. The legend surrounding the buried gold treasure has grown over the years, including that the gold could only be dug up on a night of the full moon, at midnight, and by three people.

In 1850, two men supposedly found the treasure on Charles Island, only to abandon it and run hysterically off the island because of a "screeching, flaming skeleton descending from the sky." They apparently went insane and never revealed where the treasure was. Other strange and unexplained phenomena have been happening on Charles Island for years. The Wepaowag Indians considered the island sacred and the spirits of their ancestors wandered the land there. The English settlers had other plans for the island and defeated the Wepaowags for control of the desirous island. The chief of the Wepaowags put a curse on the island to the effect that, "any shelter will crumble to the earth, and he shall be cursed."

In the late 1700s, a nonastery was built, and the monks, dismissing the island curse, proceeded to go about their work. Unfortunately a series of unexplained deaths, suicides, cases of insanity, and intense hauntings forced them to retreat from their monastery. The ruins can be seen today, along with the ruins of a Catholic retreat center from the late 1920s.

In the 1950s, an attempt to build on the island was made. A lodge and seaside restaurant was under construction when a fire roared through the buildings forcing all construction to a halt. There have been no further attempts to build since that time.

On the mainland in the 1950s, the shoreline of Silver Sands beach was being developed and the building of single-family homes was under way. Suddenly the force of "Hurricane Diane" in 1955 destroyed all 75 homes. The acquisition of the land and a plan for returning the site back to its natural interior tidal wetlands, separated from Long Island Sound by sand dunes, was later put into effect by the state.

Today Silver Sands State Park and Charles Island are open to the public, but the island interior is closed from May to August to protect heron and egret rookeries. Many hikers report seeing phantom monks, apparitions, and glowing specters, as well as hearing voices and music near the ruins on the island. Some visitors reported seeing what appeared to be an Indian Dance Festival. The ghosts appear harmless, but history warns best not to build or dig while you are visiting.

SILVER SANDS STATE PARK
ONE SAMUEL SMITH LANE
MILFORD, CONNECTICUT 06460
(203) 735-4311

MAMMOTH CAVE
KENTUCKY

Men in Black: Meet the Cave Men Who Haunt the World's Largest Tunnel

Just the thought of an underground cave sounds spooky. But, when you're talking about the longest recorded system of caves in the world, with more than 360 miles of surveyed passageways on five different levels, and then you throw in the fact that they're haunted down there, it's beyond frightening.

The tales of the wonders of Mammoth Cave have been luring curious tourists-and ghost hunters-deep into its tunnels since 1816. The fascination escalated dramatically in 1925 when amateur caver Floyd Collins was pinned by a boulder and died before rescuers could save him. That led to Mammoth Cave becoming a fully established national park in 1941. At that time, only 40 of its more than 300 miles of caves had been mapped.

There's no question that caves draw crowds of avid explorers and spelunkers. But there also seems to be something about caves that attracts the unusual, and Mammoth Cave is no exception. In addition to being the largest cave in the world, many say it's the most haunted. Throughout the years, there have been many ghosts associated with Mammoth Cave, some of whom have become well known to visitors and park employees.

One of these restless ghosts is said to be a man named Stephen Bishop, one of the most famous of the early cave guides. Bishop was a slave who began leading tours of the cave in 1838. Many of the guides at that time were slaves, but Bishop was considered the ultimate guide-many of his maps are still in use today. There are many reports of people meeting the ghost of Bishop within the dark corridors of the cave. Sightseers say he is always friendly and acts like a tour guide leading people who are lost out of the caves.

Another famous ghost is a man who had scorned his lover and had broken up with her while in the caves. Rumor has it she knew her way out of the caves but didn't show him the way. He got lost, vanished, and was never seen again. Some think he continues to haunt there today, searching for his way out of the caves. Others believe that her spirit is also there today, that she felt so guilty about abandoning her boyfriend that she comes back in search of him.

And, as the hauntings grow, the Cave Research Foundation adds new mileage daily-more miles of paths that are discovered. Establishing the cave area as an international treasure, the United Nations Educational, Scientific and Cultural Organization (UNESCO) designated the park a World Heritage Site in 1981 and an International Biosphere Reserve in 1990.

Mammoth's cave region sits atop porous limestone that draws rainwater down through sinkholes, channeling it into subterranean rivers that have sculpted, over thousands of years, the convoluted tunnels that make up Mammoth's extensive cave system. The nearby Green River casts a greenish reflection on the limestone.

Mammoth Cave National Park is located twenty miles northeast of Bowling Green, Kentucky; the park is open year-round. The caves are so popular that you need to make a reservation for a tour.

MAMMOTH CAVE NATIONAL PARK

MAMMOTH CAVE, KENTUCKY

(270) 758-2180

Spooky Cellblock Continues

to Haunt

Every Halloween, Eastern State Penitentiary, a grim former state prison, is the place to be for those looking for a ghostly time. Hundreds of people show up for the annual "Terror Behind the Walls" tour. The journeys through the haunted cells of this twelve-acre site are offered by candlelight, and are not recommended for the faint of heart.

These days, pained former prisoners are said to haunt its dark Gothic halls. Halloween visitors regularly report seeing the "Soap Lady" dressed in white in the last cell on the second floor. Other figures thought to be ghostly inmates from the prison's early days have been seen by visitors.

Indeed, the huge stone prison, with its solitary-confinement cells and thirty-foot-high walls, is allegedly teeming with caged spirits who are, after many years of confinement, anxious to get out. Watching over these imprisoned spirits is the apparition of a guard, who has been seen in the prison's high guard tower late at night.

Eastern State Penitentiary was famous for being one of the most expensive buildings ever built in the United States when it was opened in 1836. The prison was thought to be a new and novel design in prisons and inmate treatment. Architect John Haviland designed this landmark experiment in architecture and building technology to embody the latest ideas about institutional reform, civic responsibility, and criminal behavior. Its model became the blueprint for many prisons around the world.

The unique construction was built with a central hub with hallways extending from it. This required fewer guards, since they could keep an eye on all the hallways and cellblocks from one central location. The prisoners were kept isolated. Each cell had its own feed door and exercise yard, which prisoners were allowed to use for only one hour a day. There was no communication with the guards or with other prisoners. Whenever prisoners were allowed to leave their cells, they were forced to wear hoods over their heads.

The penitentiary was designated a National Historic Landmark by the federal government in 1965. It is now open for historic tours.

EASTERN STATE PENITENTIARY HISTORIC SITE

2124 FAIRMOUNT AVENUE

PHILADELPHIA, PA 19130

(215) 236-5111

Flash Your Lights Three Times and the Anson Light May Shine on You

The town of Anson, population of about 1,000, is located twenty miles north of Abilene, Texas; Anson draws large crowds, and has been the host to the television series *Unsolved Mysteries*.

The attraction at Anson is the phenomenal light, bluish in color, that many of the town residents and visitors have witnessed. The light is seen at a graveyard right outside of Anson. When you get to the graveyard, turn right on a dirt road that goes up a small hill right beside the graveyard. You follow that dirt road until you come to an intersection; at that intersection you need to turn your car around and point it in the direction of the road that passes the graveyard. Then, turn your car engine off, flash your parking lights three times, and watch as the light approaches you.

Of course the Anson Light is so popular that it is hard to view the light when there are too many cars and too many teenagers. It is also impossible to see if it is raining or if a full moon is shining. It is most often seen on clear warm summer or autumn nights.

The light when it does appear is a small, flickering beam coming towards you which gets bigger and bigger. It looks like a lantern, getting stronger as it approaches. The Anson Light is supposedly the result of a ghost, a mother who lost a son in a snowstorm. They owned a ranch in the 1800s and a blizzard trapped them in their home. Their concern for their sheep and cattle forced the son to go check on the livestock. The mother had worked out a system where the son would blink his lantern three times if he needed help. The son never returned, the body was never found, and the mother committed suicide shortly thereafter. When you flash your lights three times she comes, only to disappear about five feet from your car, when she realizes you are not her son.

Many people have experienced the light, and extensive scientific research has been performed, trying to prove it's a reflection or a hoax. The town of Anson launched two in-depth investigations in the 1950s, and then again in the 1980s. No evidence was found. The last investigation was in the early 2000s by *Unsolved Mysteries*, and again no proof was found of a natural phenomenon or a hoax.

The crossroads are actually on a private property, part of a large ranch; but, the owners don't mind visitors to the spot as long as they do not disturb the cemetery or any animals grazing near by. The local police will move visitors on their way. However, the light is still worth seeing-according to the people who have experienced the eerie vision.

While you are in Anson you might want to also check out the Haunted Bridge right outside of town. It is an old metal bridge that is said to be haunted. When you walk across it, a cold wind blows on one side but the other side is perfectly calm and warm. People have also noticed that while walking on the bridge, footsteps underneath the bridge seem to be copying your exact steps. If you drive across it, a very loud clamoring noise is heard. The haunting is attributed to a hanging victim, who either committed suicide on the bridge or was hanged there by someone else. Either way the ghost has decided to claim the bridge as his domain.

ANSON LIGHT

ANSON, TEXAS 79501

THE MARFA LIGHTS
MITCHELL FLATS, TEXAS

Spooky Lone Star Lore: The Marfa Lights Mystery

There's a mystery surrounding Mitchell Flats, located nine miles east of the City of Marfa, far out in the West Texas desert at the base of the Chianti Mountains. There lies, or rather floats, an age-old conundrum: small, ethereal, lights suspended in the air-with no apparent source, no identifiable location. They float, they ebb, they glow, and they move. And they defy explanation.

The Marfa Lights appear in the middle of the Mitchell Flats, on remains of an old World War II Air Force training base. During its prime in the mid-1940s, many of the Air Force pilots also saw the mysterious lights.

The Ghost Lights of Marfa, as they've come to be known, were first reported more than a century ago. Robert Ellison, one of the early settlers in the area, witnessed these mysterious glowing orbs in 1883. Since then, the legend and the surrounding curiosity has grown. What once was a Texas-based story of interest has captured national recognition.

What they look like depends on whom you talk to. And few have the same story. Some say the lights are pure white and constant. Others say they are colorful and mobile. Some never see more than three at a time. Others have reported seeing up to ten orbs of light dancing in the desert air. The only consensus: They definitely exist. But no one can explain their source.

An even stranger phenomenon has been known to happen after the viewing, for those who witness the Marfa Lights begin experiencing strange happenings in their own lives. The lights seem to follow them home, and begin appearing outside their bedroom windows.

A lot of newspapers have done stories on the Marfa Lights, TV stations have gone out there and recorded them, but no one has ever figured out what causes them.

From the scientific to science fiction, everyone has a theory. The Apache Indians of years past believed the eerie lights were stars dropping to earth. Some romantics describe the lights as the torches of deceased lovers wandering endlessly in search of one another. Others say that they are aliens or UFOs in the area. And some believe they are the spirits of the Indians themselves, their souls shining over their former homeland.

Many scientific experts and paranormal experts have been out there studying the lights, but, at this time, are still no explanations, only speculations. There is a Mystery Lights Festival in Marfa every Labor Day weekend. Thousands of visitors flock yearly to the small desert plain to witness the ghost lights. Few leave disappointed.

MARFA LIGHTS

NEAR MARFA, TEXAS 79843

PART IV

Meet the Rich and Famous

Who've Charted the Course for Celebrity Ghosts

Some say celebrity doesn't last forever. But for these famed actors, writers, politicians, artists, and celebs, the afterlife introduces a whole new chance for spotlight phantom performance. Here are the rich, the famous, and the noteworthy who have positioned themselves as the picture of paranormal-and their second crack at fame could be their best one yet.

With selections on such famous and infamous figures as Blackbeard, Aaron Burr, William Faulkner, Jean Harlow, Houdini, Dolley Madison, Ozzie Nelson, and Edgar Allan Poe, this collection of stories speaks volumes about the fact that every day a new ghost star is born. Or reborn.

Consider for example, that Edgar Allan Poe is alive and well as a ghost; he is said to haunt Poe House, his home in Baltimore, Maryland. While the Pirate Blackbeard continues—through his hauntings—to wreak havoc on the tranquil seaport town of Beaufort, North Carolina.

Even Hollywood has become a haunted haven for stars from movies and television. The spectral image of Marilyn Monroe appears to guests in a mirror at Hollywood's Roosevelt Hotel. America's favorite father Ozzie Nelson reportedly haunts the home where he lived for more than twenty-five years, now a private residence in the Hollywood Hills. And it's not only the stars themselves who've come back to haunt. At the Los Angeles Pet

Memorial Park, Rudolph Valentino's Great Dane, Kabar, might lick your hand when you visit.

Political sites are also buzzing with paranormal activities. The White House is perhaps the best-known residence in America. But, does every American know that the historic house at 1600 Pennsylvania Avenue is also filled with historic ghostly figures? Several rooms of the executive mansion, built to serve as the residence for the president and his family, are haunted. Some of the White House ghosts are those of U.S. presidents. Abraham Lincoln has been seen looking out onto the Potomac from a window in the Oval Office. The ghost of William Henry Harrison is frequently heard in the attic; Andrew Jackson revisits his bedroom; Thomas Jefferson is heard practicing piano.

One thing about famous ghosts is that they like their digs, and they are not about to leave. Many of these ghosts can still be found dwelling in their homes, favorite restaurants, clubs, and even in movie studios. Ghost tours usually highlight these spots on their tours.

Famous Ghosts

BLACKBEARD
BEAUFORT, NORTH CAROLINA

The Hammock House is not only the oldest house in the seaport town of Beaufort, North Carolina, it may be the most haunted house in town as well. The house is constructed in the Bahamian style of architecture common to Beaufort's older homes. The house was constructed to serve as an inn for the sailors and other travelers looking for food and lodging. Once a hideout for the infamous pirate Blackbeard and his crew, the now privately owned home keeps North Carolina's most notorious pirate's spirit alive and kicking.

According to legend, Edward Teach, better known as Blackbeard, was a guest of the inn while his ship was being reconditioned. Blackbeard is rumored to have had fourteen wives. One of them was an 18-year-old French woman; it is said that he got so angry with her that he hanged her from a tree in the backyard when he departed. She was buried right there in the yard, and her ghostly screams can now be heard on nights when the moon is bright.

Today, Hammock House is a must-stop on historic tours of Beaufort. Tour guides regale the history of Blackbeard and say his angry spirit can still be felt here in mysteriously slamming doors and "eerie" feelings felt by some of those who take the tour.

In 1862, during the Union occupation of Beaufort, three Federal officers were quartered in the Hammock House. These three men were seen entering the house one evening and never seen again—that is, until 1915 when workmen digging near Hammock House found their bodies. Their ghosts have since been seen wandering the grounds.

The Hammock House went through a long period of neglect and vandalism after the Civil War, partly because the locals believed it was haunted. Built around 1700, the two-story structure sat on a hill, or hammock, and served as a landmark to ships entering the inlet. The home has had thirty-one owners in its 300-year history.

HAMMOCK HOUSE
BEAUFORT, NORTH CAROLINA
(PRIVATE RESIDENCE)

Meet Blackbeard

Between the years of 1717 and 1718, one man's name drew terror on the seas more than any other: Blackbeard.

An imposing 6 feet, 5 inches and 220 pounds, with a long black braided beard tied in ribbons and smoldering, smoking ropes stuffed in his three-corned hat for effect, the man known as Blackbeard the Pirate struck fear in all he encountered. It is believed that Blackbeard was born as Edward Teach (aka Thatch) in London or Bristol sometime before 1690. Little is known of his early life. It is generally assumed that he started his career as a privateer employed by Queen Anne in her war with the French, Spanish, or any other enemy of the crown. When Queen Anne's War ended, Blackbeard pursued pirating.

Blackbeard plundered small ships in the Caribbean for a few years, but by May of 1717, he arrived off the coast of Charleston, South Carolina, with a fleet of four ships and possibly 400 men. After plundering ships there, he sailed north to Beaufort, North Carolina, where it appears that he intentionally grounded his ship, the *Queen Anne's Revenge*, on a sandbar.

In November of 1718, Blackbeard left Beaufort and came to his end in a raging sea battle in the Ocracoke Inlet with the British ship *Ranger*. His life was finally ended by a sword to his neck. He was beheaded, his body thrown over board, and his head was hung from the bowsprit. Before throwing his body over, they counted twenty-five major wounds to his body, a reminder of the brutal life he had led.

JOHN WILKES BOOTH
FORD'S THEATRE
WASHINGTON, D.C.

The Fugitive: Booth Continues to Haunt the Ford's Theatre Murder Scene. Or Does He?

Except for the assassination and storm of controversy surrounding the death of John F. Kennedy, there is arguably no chain of American historic events more shrouded in mystique and myth than that associated with John Wilkes Booth following the shooting of Abraham Lincoln at Ford's Theatre in Washington, D.C. The theater is now owned by the National Park Service.

Today, that mystery continues to surface as Booth's ghost continues to haunt and taunt visitors at the renovated museum and playhouse. Or does it?

Ford's Theatre may be the most famous theater in the nation. On April 14, 1865, during the performance of *Our American Cousin*, John Wilkes Booth entered Box Seven and assassinated President Abraham Lincoln. After firing the fatal shot to Lincoln's head, Booth jumped from the president's box to the stage, breaking his leg in the fall. He managed to escape the theater and days later was hiding in a barn on Richard Garret's farm near Bowling Green, Virginia, when soldiers surrounded him. They set the barn on fire, and Booth is thought to have died either in the blaze or from the accompanying gunfire.

But, the mystery remains.

Though actors, audiences, and the staff of the theater and the museum have reported seeing Booth's ghost, others argue that because of the damage to the farm where he escaped, Booth's body was never positively identified. Conspiracy theorists believe that Booth may have actually somehow escaped the carnage. But, that still doesn't explain the sightings of him at Ford's.

In addition, actors often feel an icy presence, become ill, or forget their lines when standing near the spot at the left-center stage where Booth landed. Adding to the deep mystery surrounding Booth are scores of strange facts, including:

- Booth's alcoholic father who claimed to have had "ghostly experiences."
- The ghost of Mary Surratt, said to have been one of Booth's co-conspirators in the assassination plot, and the first woman ever executed for murder in the United States, haunts the Surratt House and Tavern near Washington.
- The sergeant who claimed to have shot and killed Booth was described as being an unbalanced man "who talked directly to God."
- Many of the main characters involved in the Booth story reportedly died strange and mysterious deaths.

Lincoln's ghost has never been seen at Ford's, but it has been spotted across the street at Petersen House, where he was carried and where he subsequently died.

FORD'S THEATRE
511 10TH STREET, NW
WASHINGTON, D.C. 20004
(202) 347-4833

JOHN BROWN AND HARPERS FERRY
HARPERS FERRY, WEST VIRGINIA

John Brown's Soul Still Alive in Spirit

Born in West Torrington, Connecticut, on May 9, 1800, John Brown was born into a deeply religious family; his father Owen was an abolitionist and a stationmaster for the Underground Railroad when the family moved to Ohio. It was his father's antislavery influence that most likely inspired Brown to take an active role in the end of slavery. His passion and commitment to free slaves in the upper South ended in Brown's capture and hanging at Harpers Ferry on December 2, 1859.

His life was never easy. Married twice and with twenty children between the two families, he struggled all his life to carve out a career. First he tried taking over his father's tannery business, then sheep herding, land speculation, and the wholesale business. But, he was never very successful, and his family ended up impoverished.

Harpers Ferry was his first target in his attempt to run off large numbers of slaves. At the time, Harpers Ferry was a town filled with arms factories that stored large supplies of state-of-the-art weapons. It stands at the cusp of the Virginia split, the area between the slaveholders of the tidelands and the western Virginians who were opposed to slavery. It is believed that Brown thought the local Virginians would help him and his men, but they never came to his rescue, and he and his troops were defeated.

Today, his spirit is said to haunt his farmhouse headquarters. It is called the Kennedy Farmhouse and is a 200-year-old restored log cabin, located five miles outside the town.

Brown and his twenty-one men slept upstairs in the small attic. Witnesses have heard John Brown's ghost pace back and forth on the top two floors. Footsteps of a crowd of people can be heard going up the steps. Sounds of people talking, breathing, and snoring have been heard as well. Psychics feel an aura in the attic. One psychic claimed to have made contact with John Brown himself, who was "pleased" with the renovation work done on his old headquarters.

An apparition resembling John Brown himself has been seen walking down the streets of Harpers Ferry, occasionally smiling at a visitor. He obligingly posed for a picture with some Alabama tourists, who enthusiastically asked him to join them. When these tourists got their pictures back, there was a blank space where he had stood.

Harpers Ferry is located off U.S. Highway 340, where the

Potomac and Shenandoah Rivers meet. Today, it is a National Historic Park. A tour of the haunted places is given regularly.

In addition to Brown, many other restless spirits walk the streets of Harpers Ferry, and wander in and out of the buildings and historic homes.

HARPERS FERRY NATIONAL HISTORIC SITE

HARPERS FERRY, WEST VIRGINIA 25425

(304) 535-6029

AARON BURR

Aaron Burr Leads the Spooks of New York City

There are several ghosts and spirits that haunt New York City, especially in Greenwich Village, a popular spirit hangout. The fashionable West Village restaurant, One If by Land, Two If by Sea, is the popular haunt of Aaron Burr, the former vice president of the United States, who is now primarily remembered for killing Alexander Hamilton in a duel.

The restaurant ambiance is romantic, and lovely piano music provides the backdrop to a dining experience reminiscent of another time. But unsuspecting patrons have encountered the angry spirit of Aaron Burr, who is said to move chairs out from under guests, bump waiters serving trays, sending food and dishes crashing, create chilly air around the dining room, and wreak havoc with the fireplace.

Once a carriage house owned and operated by Burr, the Greenwich Village restaurant is also said to be haunted by Burr's daughter, Theodosia Burr Alston. As Burr's only child, she and her father were devoted to each other, and Theodosia was a source of great comfort to Burr during his long trial for treason in 1807, for which he was finally acquitted.

Apparitions of Theodosia in a flowing white dress have been seen floating through the restaurant. She'd supposedly adored beautiful jewelry and loved earrings that glittered; women sitting at the bar have remarked that they feel something tugging on their earrings.

Theodosia lived in the Carolinas with her wealthy plantation owner husband Joseph Alston, with whom she had a son, Aaron Burr Alston. After the death of her son from tropical fever at the tender age of ten, her father convinced her to come to New York. Her ship, *The Patriot* vanished without a trace off the coast of the Carolinas on December 30, 1812. Some speculated that she and the ship fell victim to coastal pirates. There are also reports of Theodosia's ghost in the same flowing white dress hovering over the water on the beach of Huntington State Park in South Carolina.

All in the Family

The Burr father and daughter duo are not the only ones whose spirits have come back to clear up unfinished business. At The Morris-Jumel Mansion, in Washington Heights, New York City, Eliza Jumel, the ex-wife of Aaron Burr and former mistress of the mansion, is said to wander around the house in a purple dress, rapping on the walls and windows. She and her first husband, Stephen Jumel, a wealthy wine merchant restored the mansion in 1810.

A British Colonel, Roger Morris, built the mansion as a gentleman's farm before the Revolutionary War. General George Washington used the mansion as his headquarters during the Long Island campaign. Today, the mansion is a popular museum and tourist destination.

A popular tale about the mansion is about a history teacher taking her class for a visit, and when she entered into a room a revolutionary war soldier appeared, as if he just stepped out of a painting on the wall. She fainted on the spot. Others have seen the soldier as well.

Eliza's first husband, Stephen Jumel, was said to be a very angry ghost. Visitors didn't see him, but talk about being pushed from behind. It was also said that objects were thrown around. A rumor that his wife had murdered him was proven true when the famous ghost hunter Hans Holzer and medium Ethel Myers conducted séances in the hopes of freeing his angry spirit. They learned that his wife had murdered him by letting him bleed to death after an accident. It is said that his spirit stopped haunting the mansion after the truth came out.

Some visitors to the mansion also report meeting the ghost of Aaron Burr, who was Eliza's second husband. After her first husband was dead, Eliza married the disgraced former vice president in the mansion's octagonal parlor in 1833. A year later, she filed for divorce against Burr, saying he squandered her money on Texas land developments and committed adultery. The divorce became final on the day of Burr's death at age 78 in 1836.

ONE IF BY LAND, TWO IF BY SEA
17 BARROW STREET
NEW YORK, NEW YORK
(212) 255-8649

THE MORRIS-JUMEL MANSION
65 JUMEL TERRACE
NEW YORK, NEW YORK
(212) 923-8008

THE BELL WITCH GHOST
ADAMS, TENNESSEE

One of American History's Most Famous Witches

It's considered one of the most famous ghost tales in American history: the Bell Witch story. The so-called Bell Witch is a sinister entity that tormented a family on Tennessee's frontier between the years of 1817 and 1821.

Adams, Tennessee, a small farming community north of Nashville near the Kentucky border, is the scene of the Bell Witch beginnings: the John Bell Farm. In the early 1800s, John Bell moved his family from North Carolina to the Red River bottomland in Robertson County, Tennessee, settling in a community that later became known as Adams. Bell purchased some land and a large log home for his family. The Bells quickly made many friends and gained prominence in the community. John Bell acquired additional land and cleared a number of fields over the next several years.

One day in 1817, John Bell was inspecting his cornfield when he encountered a strange-looking animal sitting in the middle of a cornrow. He was shocked by the appearance of this animal, which had the body of a dog and the head of a rabbit. Later that night, the Bell family began experiencing strange phenomena in their home. It started with knocking and rapping noises and scratching sounds. These mysterious sounds continued with increased force each night. Bell and his sons often hurried outside to catch the culprit but always returned empty-handed. The noises were soon followed by more problems. The Bell children began waking up frightened and complaining of sounds much like rats gnawing at their bedposts. It wasn't long until the children began complaining of more terrifying things—having their bed covers pulled and their pillows tossed onto the floor by a seemingly invisible force.

The force had an eerie presence. Some say the spooky presence belonged to the bizarre animal Bell spotted on his farm. Others argue that the spirit belongs to Kate Batts, a neighbor of the Bell family, with whom John had experienced some bad business dealings. Reportedly, Kate began making daily appearances at the Bell home to torment them. Soon, the spirit was creating havoc all through Robertson County.

The ghost was the talk of the town. It is said that John suffered from bouts of serious illness, for which the Bell Witch ghost claimed responsibility. One day, he went to bed and never woke up. At his funeral, she made herself known—laughing, cursing, and singing as the poor man was buried. But, the death of her enemy did not signal the end of Kate; she continued to stay and torment John's daughter Betsy. Eventually, she went away, but did come back again for a short period.

Even today, the infamous Bell Witch is shrouded in mystery and intrigue. Was she really a ghost? Was it poltergeist activity? Or did Kate Batt's hatred for John Bell take on a life of its own? Today, the original house is not open to the public. But, the owners offer tours of an authentic reproduction of the Bell Family cabin, complete with period furniture, and a recounting of the strange events that occurred back in the early 1800s.

THE BELL WITCH HOME AND CAVE

ADAMS, TENNESSEE

(615) 696-3055

WILLIAM FAULKNER
OXFORD, MISSISSIPPI

Even while he was alive, a mystique was forming about William Faulkner. Now, in death, the mystery continues, as the Southern writer continues to haunt and inspire both on paper and as a ghost.

Known as a difficult man, Faulkner and his writings were often equally difficult to understand. Perhaps, some say, that is why he has returned in ghostly spirit to keep attention focused on his works and inspire further understanding.

In 1930 William Faulkner purchased what was then known as "the Bailey Place," a large Greek Revival house that predated the Civil War, standing on four acres of cedars and hardwood. He later purchased the adjoining Bailey Woods. Today, he haunts the home where he lived, which is known as the Rowan Oak House; his ghost has been seen wandering the grounds and writing on a wall in one of his old rooms.

The University of Mississippi purchased the Rowan Oak House from his daughter Mrs. Jill Summers in 1973. Visitors to this historical landmark, located in the center of Oxford, Mississippi, say they hear the sounds of footsteps and piano music, and caretakers say they often enter in the morning to find things have been thrown and crashed on the floor, reminders of Faulkner's characteristic temper.

William Cuthbert Falkner (he added the "u" later) was born in New Albany, Mississippi on September 25, 1897. The Falkners were businessmen, and the same was expected of William. But various family attempts to interest him in commerce—jobs in banking and bookkeeping were among his short-lived professions—failed miserably. It proved futile, for, as he stated at the time, "money (is) a contemptible thing to work for."

Faulkner died in 1962 in Mississippi. The recognition of his talent during his life had included the Nobel Prize, the Pulitzer Prize for Literature, and the National Book Award. Arguably, he is the best writer of fiction that America has produced, and a spirited ghost with a literary past.

ROWAN OAK AND BAILEY'S WOODS

OXFORD, MISSISSIPPI

(662) 234-3284

Four's Company Plus One: Ghosts Share Home with Living

It was once a dormitory, which explains in many parts why the multitude of ghosts who still haunt the Garfield House in Ohio live comfortably with the private residence owners today.

Once home to President James Garfield, the Garfield House is perched on a hill, overlooking Garfield Road, at the edge of Hiram, Ohio, twenty-five miles southeast of Cleveland. The spirits of its former occupants continue to haunt the mansion.

Built in 1836, this Greek Revival mansion underwent many transitions, at one point serving as a boarding house for faculty members of the Western Reserve Eclectic Institute College. James Garfield was a student there from 1851 to 1854. After graduating from Williams and Mary College in 1856, Garfield returned to Western Reserve to become a teacher and principal, and then president of the school. He married Lucretia Rudolph the same year, in 1859, that he was elected to the Ohio State Senate. They continued to live in the boarding house until 1861. That year Garfield left Hiram, Ohio, to fight in the Civil War.

He would go on to become the twentieth president of the United States. He served only a few months before an embittered attorney who had been seeking a consular post shot him on July 2, 1881. He was shot in Washington, D.C., but died on Sept. 19th, 1881 in New Jersey, where he had been taken in the hopes of recovery. Perhaps his slow death, lingering for more than two months, is why his spirit clings to this world.

The mansion had several owners until 1907, when Marcia Henry, a teacher at the college, bought the place. The mansion was willed to Hiram College, where it stayed until 1961, when it was moved to its present location, where it sits today as a private residence. The ghostly spirits seem to have come to life when the house was moved. And, they've been around ever since.

Today, the ghosts of Garfield, his wife Lucretia, Marcia Henry, and another rooming- house boarder, student Almeda Booth, haunt the stately home.

Also, there is a boy ghost named Andrew, but no one is quite sure what his connection to the house is. They are all going about their business as if they never left. Frequent ghostly happenings include:

· When Garfield's name is mentioned, the dining
  room lights flicker.

- Lights in the bedrooms turning on in the early morning hours.
- Faucets start running spontaneously.
- Even in the middle of scorching hot summer days, the temperature in the mansion's kitchen can be freezing cold.
- Objects sometimes fly around the room, or move by themselves.
- Lucretia Garfield has appeared in a back bedroom upstairs, enjoying the view from its window into the backyard garden.
- The smell of cigar smoke wafts through the house. Garfield loved cigars.
- Handwritten pieces of paper in what appears to be Garfield's handwriting appear and disappear.
- The front door had a habit of opening itself, even when it was securely locked.

The common thread with the Garfield House ghosts is that they all lived in the house at one point and now seem to be willing to share the house with the living. It is believed Marcia Henry comes back because she loved the mansion when she owned it and told her relatives she would return after she died. Garfield may still feel angry about his untimely assassination and is seeking recognition.

Garfield House is a private residence and the house is located on a hill overlooking Garfield Road. There is a James Garfield National Historic Site in Lawnfield House in Mentor, Ohio. He purchased it in 1876, and after his death his wife, Lucretia, added a memorial library and vault for storing historic papers. It thus became the first presidential library and set a precedent for future presidents to build personal libraries.

THE GARFIELD HOUSE
HIRAM, OHIO

JAMES GARFIELD NATIONAL HISTORIC SITE
8095 MENTOR AVENUE
MENTOR, OHIO
(440) 255-8722

A Star is Born (Again)

Meet the Ghosts of Hollywood
Hollywood, California

Hollywood, the land of bright lights, fame, fortune and, sometimes, broken dreams. Is it any wonder that a place that inspires stardom would also inspire celebrity comebacks? Comebacks of the ghostly kind?

There are Hollywood bus tours. And there are haunted Hollywood bus tours. Many say Tinsel Town is a hotbed of the paranormal experience. That's because what is increasingly popular in recent years are excursions that introduce fans to the afterlife of their favorite stars. Here, they are given a glimpse into the ghostly encounters of such greats as Marilyn Monroe, Jean Harlow, Clifton Webb, Orson Welles, Rudolph Valentino, and Ozzie Nelson, to name a few.

MEET THE HOLLYWOOD AFTERLIFE STARS

Here's a look at some of the stars who are haunting Hollywood from their graves:

Ozzie Nelson

America's favorite TV father Ozzie Nelson reportedly haunts the home where he lived for more than twenty-five years, now a private residence, at 1822 Camino Palermo Road in the Hollywood Hills.

When Harriet Nelson sold the house in 1980, the new owners discovered many mysterious activities going on including faucets and lights that turned themselves on and off, doors that opened and closed themselves and loud footsteps upstairs when no one was there.

Although Ozzie's apparition has never been seen the owners believe that these things are the work of Nelson's spirit.

Made famous on the television show *The Adventures of Ozzie and Harriet*, Ozzie was also a former bandleader and singer. He married Harriet Hilliard, who was a singer in the band. During his life he and Harriet shared their home with their sons David and Eric "Ricky" until the sons grew up and moved out.

The Nelson TV house seen on the series (built on Stage 5 at General Service) is an exact replica of the front of their real-life home in Hollywood California, a Colonial style shingle house with green shutters.

Jean Harlow

During her lifetime, Hollywood film siren and first "blonde bombshell" Jean Harlow was known to frequently attend séances. So it's no surprise then that Harlow has made a huge comeback in the afterlife.

Many speculate that it is because her life was so short, (she died from kidney failure at the age of 26), that Harlow has come back to show Hollywood the rising star she was and could have been.

Harlow made three dozen films between 1927 and 1937, though she had only small parts in many of them. She appeared in color only once, during a short sequence in *Hell's Angels*. Even with such a brief career, she was still voted number 22 on the American Film Institute's list of the greatest actresses of the Golden Age. Never a great dramatic actress, she nevertheless had a beauty and energy that filled the screen, and her comic performances were wonderful. The

potential was there for much more. According to biographer
Eve Golden, "in the last year or two of her life she was really
starting to take charge."

According to legend, she now comes back to haunt her
former homes-the Benedict Canyon Home in Beverly Hills,
where she lived with her director husband Paul Bern before
he committed suicide, and another former home in Westwood, Los Angeles, where her parents lived. The Westwood
home is where Jean Harlow tried to commit suicide after
Paul's death. The owners of this house recount that in the
kitchen the lights go on and off by themselves, and definite
cold spots are felt both there and in the upstairs bedroom. At
times, a strong smell of women's perfume will suddenly over-
take a room. In the living room sobs can be heard, and a feeling of great sadness overcomes whoever hears it.

Both houses have reported a faint spectral vision of a floating form around the stairways. As well as the feeling of not
being alone and strange knockings. Both homes are privately
owned and do not welcome visitors.

Born Harlean Carpentier on March 3, 1911, in Kansas
City, Missouri, she later took her mother's maiden name
(leaving her mother to be forever known as "Mother Jean"),
but not before running away from home at the age of 16 to get
married, the first of several ill-fated pairings. She broke into
pictures as a teenager, but her career was going nowhere until
she was discovered by Howard Hughes and cast in *Hell's Angels*.
That hit was followed by another hit, *Platinum Blonde*, and several films with Clark Gable, all of which did very well, making
her the reigning Hollywood "sex goddess." In 1933 she
appeared in a film that was essentially a parody of her own

career, called *Bombshell*. Her death occurred during the filming of *Saratoga* (1937), and the film was completed with a double used in long shots.

The Paul Bern and Jean Harlow House Is home to Multiple Tragedies and One Ghostly Premonition

This house on Easton Drive in Benedict Canyon was the location of Paul Bern's suicide, or, as some suspect, his murder in 1932—just a few months after his marriage to Jean Harlow.

The house went on to house more tragic endings: another man committed suicide, two people drowned in the swimming pool, and a maid hung herself.

The house arguably provided one of the most disturbing hauntings in Southern California and a ghostly premonition. When "Hair Stylist to the Stars" Jay Sebring bought the house in the 1960s, he knew of its dark and troubled past. That in fact intrigued him. In 1965 the actress Sharon Tate was housesitting this residence for her good friend, owner Jay Sebring. One night, an intruder in the bedroom awakened Tate. Tate later told columnist Dick Kleiner, "I saw this creepy little man. He looked like all the descriptions I have ever read of Paul Bern." The ghost began to run around the room haphazardly, clumsily bumping into furniture and making noise.

Frightened, Tate hurried downstairs only to be confronted by the horrifying apparition of someone bound to the newel post, with his or her throat slashed. Tate later said that she somehow knew that the mutilated figure was either herself or Sebring. She often spoke of the strange occurrence and was convinced she had seen the ghost of Paul Bern.

In 1969, after Tate had married director Roman Polanski, members of the infamous Charles Manson family murdered her, Sebring, and two others in a rented house on Cielo Drive while Roman Polanski was away. Sharon was pregnant at the time. When they were found, a nylon rope hanging from a roof beam bound Tate and Sebring's bodies together. The house on Cielo Drive was torn down, and a new house was built on the site.

Clifton Webb

He is known for his Oscar nominated roles in the movies *Laura* and *The Razor's Edge*. He also starred in *Cheaper by the Dozen*, *Bells on Their Toes* and the popular role of Mr. Belvedere in a series of films. He died at the age of 77 in 1966, and was interred at the Hollywood Memorial Cemetery. Webb's restless spirit has been seen lurking in the foyer of the Abbey of Palms Mausoleum quite frequently for years. Webb might prove to be an indecisive spirit, as his ghost has also been reportedly seen at his former home in Rexford Hills in Hollywood. His unmistakable look and style are what make him so recognizable by those who say they have seen him.

At the Hollywood Roosevelt Hotel, Marilyn Monroe is said to haunt a mirror, which sits outside the elevators in the lower level. Hundreds of tourists pass the full-length mirror each day without knowing its strange history. The mirror was originally part of the furnishings in a poolside suite, which was frequently used by Marilyn Monroe at the hotel. Several people have reported seeing the image of the tragic actress reflected in the glass of this particular mirror. Upon turning around, of course, no one is there.

Also at the Hollywood Roosevelt Hotel, Montgomery Clift haunts Room 928, where staff say they hear him pacing, memorizing his movie lines, and making noises-only when the suite is unoccupied, however. Guests who have stayed in the room have noted that the phone is somehow taken off the hook even though they have not touched it.

The hotel was the location for the first Academy Awards Ceremony in the Blossom Ballroom in 1929. The ballroom has a definite cold spot about thirty inches round, which is constantly colder than the rest of the room; perhaps it's the spot where a sore loser lurks.

Rudolph Valentino

The spirit of Rudolph Valentino is said to haunt the Paramount Studios, the huge movie studios that still reside in Hollywood. The Sheik's shimmering specter has been seen floating among old garments in the costume department.

Escape Artist: Spirited in Life and Death, Houdini Lives

Today, his spirit is said to haunt the grounds of the former mansion he lived in on a four-acre plot of land in Laurel Canyon in West Hollywood. The property was said to attract occultists and paranormal types throughout the 1960s.

Houdini bought what was then billed a looming castle from the estate of a local furniture magnate and soon moved in. The house certainly fit his theatrical personality with its parapets, battlements, and spooky towers. The foundation of the mansion was honeycombed with tunnels, secret passages, and chambers. One tunnel even ran beneath what is now Laurel Canyon Road.

He was obsessed with his own death and strongly believed in the Spiritualist movement. He wanted desperately to communicate with the spirit of his dead mother.

During the time he lived in the mansion, the home was host to séances, strange experiments, and more. It is said that prior to Houdini taking up residence in the mansion, its previous owners had experienced a murder there; a death that continued to haunt the mansion and possibly cost Houdini his life, as the ghost and haunted nature of the house became his obsession and, as his focus turned to the house and its mysteries, contributed to the downturn in his career. Though the murder remains unsolved, it was thought that the owner's son killed his gay lover after being rebuked.

Harry Houdini died on Halloween, 1926, and his mansion burned down in 1958, but people say his ghost wandered the ruins of his estate. Photos taken in the early 1990s of his ruined former home showed images of people and lighted orbs among the overgrown grounds and stone outdoor stairways and grottos. Many do not believe that Houdini ever came back and that other spirits inhabited the ruins. All that is left on the property today are the memories of the former estate, the property was bulldozed and a new home was built in the mid-'90s. However rumor has it that the house is haunted and the property keeps changing hands.

Houdini was born in Budapest, Hungary, on March 24, 1874 but grew up as Erich Weiss in the small Wisconsin town of Appleton. Erich became interested in magic and stage performing. It is said that he was once apprenticed to a locksmith, where he learned to assemble and take apart locks with his eyes closed. It was a skill that would serve him well later in life. He took the name of Houdini, which was taken from the name of Robert Houdin, a famous French magician.

THE HARRY HOUDINI ESTATE

LAUREL CANYON BOULEVARD

LOS ANGELES, CALIFORNIA 90069

(HOUSE WAS TORN DOWN)

LA Story: Phantom Pets of Filmdom

Many Hollywood stars have lived on forever as ghosts. But stars are not the only ones whose fame doesn't stay buried. Many stars of the big screen and television have buried their beloved animal companions at the Los Angeles Pet Memorial Park.

Tucked away in the lush green rolling hills of Calabasas, California, the ten landscaped acres of the Los Angeles Pet Memorial Park provide a serene and peaceful resting place for more than 40,000 animal companions.

There lies Punkie Barrymore, cat of Lionel Barrymore, a childhood pet of Lauren Bacall's, and Morey Amsterdam's dog, named Pussy Cat. Adam Sandler 's beloved pit bull, Meatball, is buried there as well as Hopalong Cassidy's horse, Mary Pickford's dog, and Petey, *The Little Rascals* dog.

And, some of the animal spirits are not resting, as visitors report frequent canine and feline ghostly happenings. Several visitors to the dog cemetery report being licked by a phantom dog, or have heard panting and barking sounds.

The spirit of Rudolph Valentino's Great Dane, Kabar, is active and barking here; it may be the ghost that gets the most attention. The dog died in 1929 but has since returned as a ghost.

Like just about everything in LA, this is no ordinary dog cemetery. The park's Rainbow Garden, located near the front entrance, affords guests an opportunity for reflection in a calm, picturesque setting. One historical feature of note is the brick mausoleum, which was erected in 1929, and is the oldest original structure on the property.

Granite markers bear inscriptions in English, French, Spanish, Hebrew, Russian, Italian, and many other languages. Symbols of various religious faiths are also widely represented. Some markers bear images of beloved pets embossed on the stone. Flowers, photographs, and ornaments adorn numerous burial sites.

The park was founded and dedicated on September 4, 1928. It is, therefore, one of the oldest facilities of its kind on the West Coast. Recognizing the need for decent and dignified pet burials, the Rollins and Dr. Eugene Jones family owned and operated the facility for more than forty years. In 1973, the family graciously donated the cemetery to the Los Angeles. After managing the park for a decade, the city considered selling the property to developers.

A small group of pet owners learned of this and established S.O.P.H.I.E., Inc. ("Save Our Pets' History in Eternity"), a nonprofit public benefit corporation dedicated to the preservation of this beautiful sanctuary. S.O.P.H.I.E. members initiated a fundraising drive to purchase the grounds and lobbied at the state legislature in Sacramento to enact the first-ever state law to protect pet cemeteries. On September 12, 1986, S.O.P.H.I.E. dedicated the Los Angeles Pet Memorial Park in perpetuity.

LOS ANGELES PET MEMORIAL PARK
5068 NORTH OLD SCANDIA LANE
CALABASAS, CALIFORNIA 91372
(818) 591-7037

EDGAR ALLAN POE
BALTIMORE, MARYLAND

Edgar Allan Poe House Haunted by Grandmotherly Spirit and Mysterious Man in Black Visits Grave Yearly

Each year for more than half a century, a mysterious black-clad stranger makes a pilgrimage to the grave of Edgar Allan Poe in Baltimore's Old Western Burial Ground, leaving behind three roses and a bottle of French cognac. Wearing a black hat, black overcoat, and white scarf, he appears in the early hours of the morning every January 19th to toast the author on his birthday. No one knows the identity of the visitor or has ever guessed the origin or true meaning of the ritual at the grave where Poe lies buried alongside his wife, Virginia, and his aunt Maria Clemm. A crowd sometimes gathers outside the brick wall to catch a glimpse of the visitor.

Since he died on October 7, 1849, the living have kept the famous writer's spirit alive, but Edgar Allan Poe himself is active as well-as a ghost. Apparitions are said to haunt the Edgar Allan Poe House in Baltimore, which was built around 1830 in what was then the country. Poe's aunt Maria Clemm rented it in 1832. Poe lived there with his grandmother, aunt, and two cousins until 1835. Virginia Clemm, who later became his wife, was one of the cousins living there.

In the 1930s the Poe house was scheduled for demolition as part of a housing project but public interest forced the Housing Authority to spare the site. The Edgar Allan Poe Society was given control of the house and it opened as the Edgar Allan Poe House in 1949.

The Commission for Historic and Architectural Preservation (CHAP), a city agency, now maintains the site as a historic house museum, and sponsors tours and activities throughout the year. Many of the curators of the museum and neighbors report a candle-like light that goes from floor to floor when the museum is closed at night. Doors and windows open and close by themselves and an apparition of an old heavy-set women in 1830s-style clothing has been seen in the upstairs bedroom, where Poe's grandmother died.

In 1836, Poe married his 13-year-old cousin, Virginia. Poe was devoted to his wife. When she died a tragic death from consumption in 1847, a painting of her was done from her corpse and hangs in the museum. Poe outlived her by only two years; the cause of his death remains a mystery. Each year at Halloween a special ceremony is held at Poe House to honor Poe, and it is said his spirit is always felt during the event.

Poe was born in Boston on January 19, 1809; he was the grandson of Baltimore Revolutionary War patriot, David Poe Sr. He was orphaned at three, but raised by Mr. and Mrs. John Allan in Richmond. It is said that Poe was never fully accepted by Allan as his son and the two had a strained relationship. Many of Poe's works have a death theme, and both the modern detective story and the modern horror novel have been attributed to him.

EDGAR ALLAN POE HOUSE
203 N. AMITY STREET
BALTIMORE, MARYLAND 21223
(410) 396-7932

EDGAR ALLAN POE MEMORIAL GRAVE
519 WEST FAYETTE STREET
BALTIMORE, MARYLAND 21201
(410) 706-2072

The White House

It's probably the best-known house in America. But it's unsure if every American knows that the historic house at 1600 Pennsylvania Avenue in Washington, D.C.-the White House-is filled with historic ghostly figures. Several rooms of the executive mansion, which was built to serve as the residence of the president of the United States, are haunted.

Many of the White House ghosts are those of U.S. presidents. Abe Lincoln is one of the ghosts believed to be wandering around the house The ghost of William Henry Harrison is frequently heard in the attic. Andrew Jackson revisits his bedroom in what is now called the Queen's Bedroom; definite cold spots are felt and his laughter has been heard there. Thomas Jefferson has been heard practicing piano. And there are more.

First Lady of the Hauntings

She was a First Lady. And she was *the* first lady-of haunt-ings, that is. Abigail Adams, wife of President John Adams, is the first known spirit to haunt the White House. From 1797 to 1801 she was the First Lady of the White House. And, after her death, she became the first spirit to be recorded as being seen at the White House.

During her time there, Abigail would hang her wash to dry in the East Room; she was drawn to the room for its warmth and bright sunlight. These days, her ghostly spirit has been seen many times and by many people hanging up her laundry in the East Room or on her way there. She is seen carrying what appears to be stacks of cloths on her out-stretched arms. The room sometimes smells of soapy water and damp clothes.

Abigail was the second daughter of four children born to the Rev. William Smith and Elizabeth Quincy in Weymouth, Massachusetts. Abigail was thought to be too sickly to go to school, so she learned to read by having her older relatives help teach her. Fortunately, her family had good libraries, so she read the Bible and the works of Milton, Locke, Shakespeare, and others.

The Adams children included: Abigail "Nabby," John Quincy, Susanna (died at 14 months), Charles, Thomas Boylston, and one stillborn daughter. Their first home was in Braintree (now Quincy) Massachusetts, where they had a farm. While John was away for business or government, she managed the home and farm with the help of servants.

Some say though her happiest times were in the newly built White House, and that is why she still continues her washing chores in the East Room.

DOLLEY MADISON

A Rose Is a Rose. . . Dolley Madison's Spirit Protects White House Garden

One of the most popular White House ghosts is Dolley Madison. The ghost of the former First Lady hovers over and protects a rose garden she planted there decades ago. It is said that when Mrs. Woodrow Wilson wanted the garden moved and parts destroyed, Dolley's figure appeared in front of the workers, scaring them and anyone else trying to mess with her flowers. To this day, the Rose Garden remains very much as she left it.

Though the White House gardens, and particularly her beloved Rose Garden, are her regular haunts, Dolley has been known to venture away from the gardens and visit some of her other favorite spots. The ghost of Dolley Madison can still be seen from time to time sitting in a rocking chair on the front porch of a house she occupied in Lafayette Park later in life. She also makes frequent appearances at the nearby Octagon House and Halcyon House, which are also haunted houses in Washington, D.C.

Abraham Lincoln
The White House

Security Check: Abe Lincoln Continues to Keep Watch on America

During times of turmoil in the United States, Abraham Lincoln is said to send his inspiration and spirit back to the White House to watch over his beloved country.

It's said Lincoln strides up and down the second floor hallway, raps at doors, and is often seen standing by the window with his hands clasped behind his back. There are numerous accounts from maids and butlers throughout the history of the White House swearing they have seen Lincoln's ghost.

On a state visit, Queen Wilhelmina of the Netherlands stayed in the Rose Room and reported hearing footsteps and a knock on her door. She opened it to find Abraham Lincoln, in a frock, topcoat, and a top hat, standing before her. She fainted.

One of the first people to have seen Lincoln in the White House was Grace Coolidge, the wife of President Calvin Coolidge; she saw Lincoln's silhouette standing at one of the windows in the Oval Office, looking out at the Potomac. Others have reported seeing him in the same pose.

Presidents Theodore Roosevelt, Herbert Hoover, and Harry S Truman all heard unexplained knocks on their bedroom door, which they attributed to Lincoln. President Truman's daughter, Margaret, claimed to have seen Lincoln's ghost. A bodyguard to President Harrison was kept awake many nights trying to protect the president from mysterious footsteps he heard in the hall. Lincoln has been sighted most often in the room now known as the Lincoln Bedroom.

One staff member claimed to have seen Lincoln sitting on his bed pulling on his boots; other staff members will not go into the Lincoln Bedroom or near that part of the White House because they feel it is too spooky. Ronald Reagan's daughter Maureen said she saw apparitions in the Lincoln Bedroom; her father's dog would bark at the door to the room but would not go in. Many overnight guests have reported hearing his phantom footsteps in the hall outside of the Lincoln Bedroom

Eleanor Roosevelt claimed that she often sensed Lincoln's presence while she was working at her desk but she never saw him. She said that she found his presence reassuring.

When Jackie Kennedy was asked by reporters she said she felt his presence and "took great comfort in it".

Mary Todd Lincoln had a great interest in the Spiritualist movement of the mid-nineteenth century, and she became friendly with mediums, especially the Lauries of Georgetown. During the Lincoln years there were many séances in the White House; although Lincoln was not a believer the way his wife was. She wanted desperately to connect to her deceased sons Willie and Eddie; she believed she had done so, as well as speaking to the ghost of President John Tyler.

THE WHITE HOUSE

1600 PENNSYLVANIA AVENUE, NW

WASHINGTON, D.C. 20500

(202) 456-1414

WASHINGTON, D.C.

The Octagon House

This house was built in 1799 by Colonel John Tahoe and was used by President Madison as his home after the burning of the White House. The home was witness to the tragic death of Tahoe's pregnant daughter, who jumped from the top banister railing into the marble foyer after her father banished her soldier lover. Her ghost still roams the house, moaning, and cold spots are felt near where she threw herself. Her father also haunts the house.

The Renaissance Mayflower Hotel

This hotel hosted its first Inaugural Ball on March 4, 1925. But, Calvin Coolidge did not attend his own Inaugural Ball because he was in mourning, as his sixteen-year-old son had recently died from blood poisoning. Since that time, the hotel started having very strange occurrences the night of the Inaugural Ball; the lights dim and flicker around 10:00 p.m., the time Coolidge's pending arrival would have been announced. An elevator that would have transported him to the ball will not move until 10:15-electricians have checked but do not find any electrical problems.

Perhaps President Coolidge is finally enjoying his Inaugural Ball.

The Hay-Adams Hotel

The Hay-Adams Hotel was built in 1927 on the site of presidential advisor Henry Adams's mansion, which was built in 1880. His wife, Marian Hooper Adams had been found dead in the mansion. Her body was discovered in front of the fireplace, but it is not known how she died. These days, her ghostly floating figure has been seen throughout the hotel. The smell of mimosa is in the air on the hotel's eighth floor. A sixth-floor housekeeping closet will never stay locked, and staff have reported seeing Mrs. Adams hovering around the door. In 1997, all the doors of the second floor guest rooms opened at once, causing the head of security great angst. They attributed these occurrences to Marian Hooper Adams.

Marian Hooper Adams is buried in Washington's Rock Creek Cemetery; her tombstone is that of a hooded woman designed by Augustus Saint-Gaudens. This statue is called "Grief," and anyone standing in front of it will begin to cry and feel a great sense of loss.

A Profile of Abraham Lincoln

Abraham Lincoln was born on February 12, 1809 in Hardin County, Kentucky. The son of a frontiersman, Lincoln had to struggle for a living and for learning. His mother died when he was ten, and his father moved the family to Indiana. Lincoln made extraordinary efforts to attain knowledge while working on a farm, splitting rails for fences, and keeping store at New Salem, Illinois. Later, he served as a captain in the Black Hawk War, then spent eight years in the Illinois legislature, and rode the circuit of courts for many years. His law partner once said of him, "His ambition was a little engine that knew no rest."

He married Mary Todd, and they had four boys, only one of whom lived to maturity. In 1858, Lincoln ran against Stephen A. Douglas for senator. He lost the election, but in his debates with Douglas he gained a national reputation, which led to him becoming the Republican candidate for President in 1860.

As president, he was the head of the United States during the Civil War. In 1863, he issued the Emancipation Proclamation that declared forever free those slaves within the Confederacy.

Lincoln never let the world forget that the Civil War involved an even larger issue. This he stated most movingly in dedicating the military cemetery at Gettysburg: "that we here highly resolve that these dead shall not have died in vain-that this nation, under God, shall have a new birth of freedom-and that government of the people, by the people, for the people, shall not perish from the earth."

Lincoln won re-election in 1864, as Union military tri

A Profile of Abraham Lincoln (cont.)

umphs heralded an end to the war. The spirit that guided him was clearly that of his Second Inaugural Address, now inscribed on one wall of the Lincoln Memorial in Washington, D.C.: "With malice toward none; with charity for all; with firmness in the right, as God gives us to see the right, let us strive on to finish the work we are in; to bind up the nation's wounds."

On Good Friday, April 14, 1865, John Wilkes Booth assassinated President Lincoln at Ford's Theatre in Washington.

Resources

Special Thanks to:

The Hotel Del Coronado: Meg Kruse, Spa Director and Lauren Ash Domoho, Director of Public Relations

The Hotel Baker: Jay Perri, co-owner

The Biltmore Hotel: Linda Spitzer, storyteller, and Nancy Myers, psychic

The Jekyll Island Club: Sue Anderson, Director of Public Relations and Guest Programs

The Lodge at Cloudcraft: Pat Burunda, Office Manager

The Mason House Inn: Joy and Chuck Hanson, owners, and C.F. Dedman

The Oatman Hotel: Tom Woodward, President of the Oatman Gold Road Chamber of Commerce, and Peg Robertson, photographer and local ghost guru

The Queen Mary: Peter James and the "Ghost Encounters" Tours

The East Alabama Ghost Hunters Group: Corey Seahorn, Director and Owner

Craig Niedermaier, graphic artist and Chicago-based amateur ghost expert

Also, thank you to the managers and staff of: the Artisan Inn, the Brookdale Lodge, the Crescent Hotel and Spa, the Don CeSar Beach Resort and Spa, the Goldfield Hotel, and the Monte Vista Hotel.

Archives

Atlantic Journal Constitution Archives
Chicago Tribune Archives
Columbia College City Beat Newspapers
Eastland Disaster Historical Society
Eastland Memorial Society Archives
Gettysburg Tour Headquarters
Los Angeles Times Archives
New London Ledge Lighthouse Foundation
Orlando Sentinel Archives
State Library of Louisiana Archives

Books

Cohen, Daniel, The Encyclopedia of Ghosts, Dorset Press, 1984

Coleman, Christopher, Ghosts and Haunts of the Civil War, Barnes & Noble, 1999

Hauck, Dennis William, National Directory of Haunted Places, Penguin, 1994

Holzer, Hans, Great American Ghost Stories, Barnes & Noble, 1990

Kaczmarek, Dale, Windy City Ghosts I and II, Whitechapel Productions, 2000, 2001

Kerman, Frances, Ghostly Encounters, America's Haunted Inns and Hotels, Warner Books, 2002

Rich, Jason, The Everything Ghost Book, Adams Media, 2001

Rule, Leslie, Coast To Coast Ghosts, Andrews McMeel, 2001

Rhyne, Nancy, Coastal Ghosts, Sandlapper Publishing, 1989

Smith, Barbara, Ghost Stories of Washington State, Lone Pine, 2000

Taylor, Troy, Field Guide to Haunted Graveyards, Whitechapel Production Press, 2003

Thay, Edrick, Ghost Stories of Indiana, Ghost House, 2001

Zepke, Terrance, Ghosts of the Carolina Coasts, Pineapple Press, 1999

Web Sites:

www.AllAboutGhosts.com

www.artsandmusicpa.com

www.beneathlosangles.com

www.cielodrive.com

www.eastlanddisaster.org

www.ghostresearch.org

www.hauntedhouses.com

www.hauntedplaces.com

www.historictrust.org

www.lapetcemetery.com

www.legendsofamerica.com

www.medina.lib.oh.us

www.morrisjumel.org

www.ngeorgia.com

www.nps.gov

www.paranormal.about.com

www.pittsburghghosts.com

www.prarieghosts.com

www.sentinelpublications.com

www.theflagship/coldspot/docs.net

www.theshadowlands.net

www.whitehouse.gov

www.willardlibrary.com

Index